A RIBBON OF ROAD

IN THE MOONLIGHT

by

Michael Pearson

Paperback ISBN 9781904312635
Published in the UK by MX Publishing
335 Princess Park Manor, Royal Drive, London, N11 3GX
www.mx-publishing.co.uk

To Surfer-mädchen

Mike Brookes drove the sleek sports car through the big open wrought iron gates and pulled into the Managing Director's parking space. He sat for a moment and smiled to himself. Getting out of the car he closed the door and looked at the factory as he did every morning, as if not quite believing it. The name on the car was Pegasus Seafire and the name above the factory gate was Pegasus Cars. It was his car and his factory. He made sports cars, and approaching the end of this Year of Our Lord nineteen hundred and fifty five he had decided that it was time they went motor racing.

Actually it was a little more complicated than that. With international crises following one after the other and the latest, this Suez business, still brewing, people were nervous and sales were slow. True Pegasus were now selling a few cars in the United States, but for the most part they relied on the home market. What Mike Brookes needed was to launch his cars on an international scale, compete with the likes of Mercedes, Ferrari, and Maserati, and for that he not only *wanted* to go racing he *needed* to go racing. Without the financial backing of the larger concerns, if business did not pick up Pegasus could easily go under. His intention was to enter the World Sports Car Championship, for which he had privately been working on a design for a racing version of the car that he drove to work that morning, but initially planned to compete in a single high profile road race. Briefly he considered the Mille Miglia, the 1000 mile road race around Italy, but for a number of reasons finally settled on Sicily's Targa Florio as Pegasus' first competitive outing. Brookes realised that the Targa was an exceptionally tough race, 447 miles or some 720 kilometres long, but it suited his purposes perfectly, with laps on the public roads of something over forty miles each the long flat-out straight along the coast would display pure power, while the gruelling car breaking section through the Madonie Mountains would showcase strength and road holding. If he could win that the rest of the Sports Car Championship should be a piece of cake. The only drawback that he could see with the racing programme was that he did not have the faintest idea how he was going finance it. And he did not have an engine for the racer. And a tyre contract, he needed a tyre contract. However, as an automotive designer and engineer of considerable talent, what he did have was a chassis design that would look pretty much like the road car, but underneath would contain enough innovations for him to be confident that he could take on his illustrious competitors and hand out a few surprises.

He liked to call his premises a factory although that was a bit grand. Established in the hangars of what had been a World War II airfield in Essex, what it actually comprised was two workshops, the first a large two story affair in which the Pegasus Seafire was hand built, and the second an adjoining hangar in which the component parts for Pegasus second model, the Swift, were packaged. The Swift was a smaller vehicle, but with superb road holding and nippy acceleration was proving popular. The car also benefited from a significant financial attraction in that it sold in kit form and so avoided crippling purchase tax. It was in fact sales of the Swift that were keeping Pegasus afloat, but Brookes burning ambition was to get into the big leagues.

Reaching over to the passenger seat of the car Brookes picked up the briefcase and started toward the factory. As he neared the open double gates he could see a dozen examples of the Seafire in various stages of construction. There was room for more, but they did not have the orders at present. Walking through the gates he waved a cheery hello at the mechanics at work on the cars, and caught again the familiar smell of cellulose paint, petrol, and engine oil that he loved so much. Turning right he passed the small reception office and waved a greeting at Jeanine, the pretty young receptionist. Mounting a steel staircase to the second level he walked along a gangway that ran the length of the building to offices at the back. Stepping into his own small office he sat behind the desk and glanced at the picture of Nicola. She was the reason he was late this morning, and he smiled at the memory.

Laying the briefcase on the desk he took out his drawings for the racer and spread them out. There was a belief, almost a superstition, in motor racing that if a car looked right it was right, and this car looked right. As with the Seafire road going version, sleek aerodynamic bodywork sloped gracefully from the front up over the engine bay and gently undulating front wheel arches with their faired-in headlights, to culminate with two small fins rising just behind driver and passenger seats to border the boot and slide with silky grace over rear wheel arches to the tail end of the car.

Brookes heard a movement in the next office, rolled up the drawings, stepped to the interconnecting door and opened it. "'Morning Mark ", he said. Mark Spall, Pegasus Finance Director, looked around from the filing cabinet at which he stood. "'Morning", he replied. The two men were both in their late thirties, but while Brookes was tall with straight hair, fair almost to the point of being blonde, Spall was shorter with dark curly hair and a dark moustache. The Finance Director had been with the company for nearly two years and when not entertaining his latest female conquest, (he was single and happy with the arrangement), could still find himself lying awake at night staring at the ceiling and wondering just how it was that he came to be working for this small struggling sports car company. On leaving school he joined the Midland Bank, and, via a spell in the Army, rose steadily in the bank's hierarchy and looked forward to a steady career in banking. Then one fateful morning he found himself sent along to Pegasus to discuss what, to the bank, appeared to be the company's main area of growth - its overdraft. Spall walked into the factory and was instantly captivated by the tangible sense of excitement that seemed to hang in the very air, the sheer positive effort that went into getting the company from one day to the next, like 'seat of the pants' driving, Mike Brookes called it. Coming from the stultified world of banking, where everything was reduced to what Spall was already coming to appreciate as a faintly ludicrous scrabble for more and more money, the sheer enthusiasm that everybody at Pegasus showed to make the best cars in their field was intoxicating. Half won over already it only needed Brookes to turn on his infamous charm and the deed was done. Spall walked into the factory with grim faced warnings of dire consequences and walked out with a silly grin and a new job. Since that time the Swift had come on stream and thanks to that and his own hands at the financial wheel Pegasus looked a little healthier, but this morning the Finance Director was to be the recipient of another of those 'Brookes Specials' that he came to look forward to and dread in equal measure.

"Got a minute Mark?" asked Brookes, "something I want to show you", and so saying he opened the drawings on Spall's desk. "Something I've been working on at home", he explained. "What's this?" asked the technically challenged Finance Director, stooping over the drawings, "looks like the Seafire".

"It is in a way", said Brookes, "but this is the racing version".

"Racing version?" asked Spall with that feeling in the pit of his stomach that he wasn't going to like what was coming.

"Yes", continued Brookes, "we're going motor racing".

"Motor Racing!" exclaimed Spall, "Look, Mike, I know you've done some race driving, and were pretty good at it, but entering the Seafire in a few club meetings isn't going to help sales, which I presume is what this is all about?"

"That is what this is about, and I agree with you, entering the Seafire in a few club meetings won't help. That's why we're going to contest the Targa Florio in 1957, followed by a full World Sports Car Championship campaign in 'fifty eight..."

"The Targa Florio in fifty-seven!?" Spall sat down. "But how...?" he continued lamely. Brookes tapped the drawings, "I've designed a racing version of the Seafire that I'm convinced can win". With all his natural enthusiasm bursting through he brushed aside Spall's reservations, "we do away with the box steel chassis on the road car", he enthused, "and build a space frame. Much lighter and more rigid, we also lengthen and widen the wheel base to improve road holding for competition, plus one or two other ideas I've got." The technical details went largely over Spall's head, which was probably just as

9

well, otherwise he would have known that spaceframe technology, developed for the air industry, promised much for motor racing but was as yet pretty well untried in cars pushing out the sort of power that Brookes had in mind. One thing, however, stared him straight in the face. He swallowed, "how the hell are we going to pay for it!?" he asked. "Don't ask me", said Brookes, "that's you're job! I'm going to have my work cut out finding a competitive engine and tyres for the thing. Let me know what finance options you can come up with as soon as possible". With that he scooped up the drawings and turned back toward his office. Reaching the door he looked back over his shoulder. "Mark", he repeated, "I want the car ready to enter the Targa Florio in the spring of fifty-seven, so get your skates on, find me some money!"

"Mike, are you mad! That's not much more then eighteen months away! It can't be done!"

"It *can* be done", Brookes said firmly, "and it *will* be done. I have a letter from Vincenzo Florio accepting our entry". Stepping into his office he closed the door, and Spall put head in hands and groaned. Standing on his side of the door Brookes glanced through the window between the offices and smiled ruefully.

Sitting back at his desk he spread the drawings out once more and pored over them, checking them again, although he had already done so a dozen times. It could win, he *knew* it could win! The ringing of the telephone interrupted his thoughts and he picked up the receiver. "Hello, Mike Brookes", he said. "Hello Mike Brookes", said the sultry voice he knew so well. "Nicola", he said, "where are you? It must be all of two hours since I last spoke to you".

"I'm at work, where do you think? And I don't think I like your tone", she said in mock indignation "you sound as if I shouldn't call you".

"Not a bit of it, I was just going to say that two hours is far too long".

"That's better. Did you tell Mark about the race car?" Brookes smiled and glanced at the interconnecting door. "I did", he said. "And how did he take it?" She asked. Brookes chuckled, "he's sitting next door with his head in his hands".

"He worries too much", said Nicola. "What's the latest girlfriend like?" she queried with a woman's natural inquisitiveness for relationships. "Oh you know Mark", replied her fiancé with a man's natural eye for the obvious, "blonde, buxom..."

"Bimbo", cut in Nicola caustically. "That's a bit harsh", responded Brookes, "she's probably a very nice girl". He shifted around in his chair to look out of the window. "Now", he said, "you didn't call to ask me that, what's up?"

"Promise you won't be angry", she said.

"Of course not, what is it?"

"Well, my mother 'phoned". Brookes winced. "Yes", he asked carefully, "and...?" There was humour in her voice as she replied, "she telephoned especially with important news".

"Oh? What?"

"She telephoned *just* to tell me she heard on the radio this morning that Grace Kelly is to be engaged to Prince Rainier, and they're going to be *married within the year!*"

"Oh God", he said, "I mean oh good".

"Mike, don't be like that, she only wants the best for us. We've been engaged for over a year and she and pop just want to know when we're going to tie the knot".

11

"Yes I know they do, but I suspect that Grace Kelly and Prince what's-his-name won't be scratching round to find the mortgage money every month! I just want the business to be a little more soundly based before we take the plunge". Nicola sounded resigned, "yes I know, and I'm not getting at you, really I'm not, but you know mum. Perhaps we should invite them over".

"Of course, but you know what will happen, your mother will start in on how it really is about time you gave up work, and how *lovely* it would be for them to have grandchildren, and your father will sit me down and explain patiently and at length how it's all very well for me to build these pretty little cars as a hobby, but at my age I should be thinking about getting a *real* job..."

"I know, mum says he wants you to join his firm in The City".

"Yes I thought as much, but honestly, can you see me in pinstripes and a bloody bowler!" She chuckled that delicious throaty chuckle of hers, "well no", she said, "and anyway, I like the pretty little cars you build"

"Perhaps we should swap jobs", he said, "you build the cars and I'll be the legal whiz kid".

"It wouldn't work. I wouldn't know where to start with the cars and you'd be bored rigid being a solicitor. I'll fix something up with them, you just remember to turn on that famous charm of yours and we'll be fine".

On conclusion of the late unpleasantness, which Alan Francis spent, as he liked to put it, 'chasing the Nips across Burma', he left the Royal Engineers and took any job he could get while he put himself through college and obtained a first rate engineering degree, upon receipt of which he set up Grove Engineering with the prime purpose of gratifying his passion for performance car engines. The business operated from Leyton, his home borough in east London, occupying two arches under the main railway line that ran from Essex into the centre of the capital. This bright but frosty winter's morning Alan stood cleaning a cylinder head, although 'stood' barely describes the stylish hip swinging gyrations that he indulged in to keep warm while Elvis Presley rocked the Jailhouse on the radio. "'Morning Alan" said a familiar voice, and Francis turned toward the open door. "Brooksie!" he exclaimed and the two men stepped toward each other and shook hands warmly. "Have a cup of char", offered the engineer, "it'll warm you up", and Mike Brookes nodded his agreement. Francis poured out two steaming brews, added milk and sugar and handed one to his companion, who took a sip and grimaced. "Bloody hell", he exclaimed, "what did you stew this in, an old engine block!"

"Get it down you", replied Francis, smiling and stepping to the open door. Across the road The Crown and Anchor had stood for seventy-odd years, until that day in 1944 when the 'doodlebug' engine cut overhead and the flying bomb plunged to earth to destroy the pub and those inside. The bomb site had been cleared of much of the rubble and the cellar filled in, but the scar remained on the landscape, as did so many across Europe. Brookes had parked the Seafire where once revellers had propped up the public bar. "See you came in that rotten old machine of yours", Francis said, eyeing the sports car. "Better keep an eye on it", he continued over his shoulder, "or the oiks around here will have the wheels off it!"

"Well", said Brookes, "as one oik to another, what was the urgent 'phone call about?" Alan Francis took a drink from his cup and turned back. "You remember you told me you were taking Pegasus into motor racing?" he asked, "and you wanted me to be on the look out for an engine?"

"Yes, what...?"

"Have you thought about the Coventry Climax?"

"Yes of course," replied Brookes a little impatiently, that being the most successful British engine currently in motor racing, "it's a good unit but I don't think it will have the 'grunt' to take on the three litre Ferraris and Maseratis. Besides, it's bloody expensive".

"Yes", said Francis, enjoying the wind-up, "If I remember the requirements correctly, your engine has to be powerful..."

"Right".

"...reliable..."

"Right again".

"...and cheap".

"Yes", said Brookes, only half joking, "what I need is a race winning engine that's free".

"Well I might have just the thing", said Alan Francis, and Brookes choked, spraying his companion with tea.   With that elaborate air of someone in possession of important knowledge that his companion wants but does not have, Francis made a great show of brushing down his oily overalls.   "What the hell are you on about?" gasped Mike Brookes, recovering his composure.   His companion decided to savour the moment and so took the scenic route to the answer.   "What", he asked "do you think of the Lynx Monaco?"

"Nice car, good quality four-seater saloon, middle of the Lynx range, why?"

"And what", continued Francis, "about the engine?"

"In-line four cylinder, fifteen hundred c.c. - any chance you might be getting to the point?" replied Brookes, his

14

impatience mounting. "I've made a study of that engine", continued Francis, warming to his subject, "and its a little beauty. For a start it has a light alloy block, perfect for racing, massive weight savings, and then there's..."

"Oh for crying out loud, you've dangled the bloody carrot, get on with it!"

"I reckon", said Francis, "I could mate two of those Monaco blocks, and using a common-plane crankshaft, come up with a three litre V8 that would push out comfortably over three hundred BHP". Francis stood back and waited for the plaudits. "And", responded Brookes, occupying a plaudit-free zone, "you're going to do all this for nothing. Won the pools have you?" Alan Francis smiled, and Brookes slapped his forehead with frustration. "Dammit get on with it, will you!?" he exclaimed. "We let Lynx pay for it", said the engineer, with studied nonchalance. "Lynx!" responded Brookes, "why the bloody hell should they pay for it? They have no interest in motor racing; never have had as far as I can remember!" Alan Francis began to pace up and down, and suppressing his excitement tried to order his thoughts so as to make them coherent. If he babbled, Brookes would likely explode with frustration. "Look", he said, "Lynx are a big company, right?"

"Right, they're the biggest motor manufacturer in the country".

"Well, I have a contact in the engineering department and he tells me that there's a buzz around the company that they might be preparing to build a race car of their own, but they've not made up their minds yet whether it's to be a sports car or a Formula 1 single-seater".

"Are you sure about this?" asked Brookes, catching a glimmer of the possibilities. "It's a rumour", continued Francis, "but one that makes sense. The U.K. and Europe have been in the doldrums since the depression back in the thirties, then the bloody war came along, and then the bloody post-war rationing. People are fed up with it; they're beginning to get a little spare cash to spend at last and they want a few luxuries and a bit of excitement. I'm told that, so the reasoning goes, Lynx will get into racing in order to develop a range of sporty good quality road cars, nippy jobs with decent handling to appeal to hubby, but with four seats so he can take the wife and kids to the shops..."

"And there's nothing like racing success to promote the range" interrupted Brookes, "but why should they build an engine and give it to us?"

"I know their engineering boys, they're good at building engines for road cars, but they wouldn't know where to start with a racer. I do, I've been squeezing extra horse power out of the Ford Ten and MG engines you use in your road cars since you started, and I've had Swift owners come to me to prepare their cars for racing..."

"Yes, I'd noticed, but even so..."

"Mike, they give us the engine because we can save them invaluable time. You say you can have your car ready for the Targa Florio in spring 1957, which is under two years from now..."

"OK", Brookes mused thoughtfully, "as you see it, they will use my chassis as a test bed for their racing engine, which will give them a good couple of year's head start". Warming to the idea Brookes continued developing his thoughts out loud. "With no racing background, if they began from scratch now it would take them at least three years to develop a competitive engine *and* a chassis, maybe more. They could go racing before then but they'd take a hammering while they sorted out all the problems and that's no good for their road car image. This way *we* do all the development work, and if Lynx can see the promotional advantages to be had from motor racing you can damn well bet that so do Ford, General Motors, Renault and every other bugger who's in competition with them!" Brookes ran a hand through his hair and his glance flicked to the ceiling and back, "I mean, damn it all", he said, "That's my own thinking, that's why I want a racing pedigree for Pegasus!"

"So what do you think?" asked Francis, "do we approach them?"

"Look, Alan, you're a bloody marvel with engines but you've never built a performance job of your own before, are you sure you can do it?"

"Yes, I'm sure. I've been working on a racing design based on the Monaco engine since Lynx put the car on the market a year ago. I just didn't know what I was going to do with it. In fact if you hadn't told me that you were taking Pegasus into racing, I was seriously thinking of suggesting it to you!" Francis stepped close, looked Brookes in the eye and tapped a finger against his companion's chest. "Look", he said seriously, "if this works out you will get your engine and with any luck it will cost you little or nothing, but I'll be honest with you, that doesn't mean there will be no risk. The bloody thing might not work, there's no denying it, but I know my design and I know that it will be at least as good and probably better than anything else out there, and I can't see any other way for you to get a competitive power unit without having to pay through the nose for it!" It took a fraction of a second for Brookes to make up his mind. "You're right", he said, "Let's set up a meet with Lynx!" and the two shook hands.

2

With the hood up to keep out the relentless snow, and with Alan Francis in the passenger seat, Mike Brookes drove the Seafire to Birmingham and the headquarters of The Lynx Motor Company.   With the original building bombed flat a new state-of-the-art glass fronted factory had risen in its place, and Brookes and Francis could not fail to be impressed as they came to a halt in the car park and stepped out of the sports car.

On entering the cavernous reception area in the dedicated office block the two men approached the reception desk, and Brookes informed the receptionist that they had an appointment with The Chairman.   The receptionist picked up the internal telephone, spoke briefly, confirmed the appointment and asked them to proceed to the lift at the far end of the group of four to which she directed them.   They were to proceed to the fifteenth floor where the P.A., Ms Jameson, would meet them.

With an air of brusque efficiency, the sternly attractive Ms Jameson duly showed them to the plush main boardroom, all mahogany panelling and real leather upholstery, where Sir Charles Standish and three other company big-wheels awaited them.   Quickly appraising them, Alan Francis knew that he and his companion were in for a grilling, and hoped that Mike Brookes would be able to curb his natural impatience and inborn desire to 'get on with it'. Standish, tall, portly, in his sixties, introduced his companions, Archibald Rhead, fifties, pinstripes and pince-nez, Chief Accountant, Harold Cooper, fifties, lounge suit, Head of Engineering, and Stephen Ryan, forties, lounge suit, Chief Designer.   Standish then waved them to the large boardroom table, where the four Lynx directors sat imperiously along one side, Brookes noticing that the accountant sat at the Chairman's immediate right. That was a bad sign; he either ran the company or thought he did. Brookes recalled a pungent comment made by a self-made multi millionaire Hong Kong ship owner - accountants should be on tap, not on top. The two visitors, with a feeling that they were viewed a little like troublesome schoolboys, were seated at the other side of the table.

Sir Charles Standish opened the meeting by hefting a sheaf of papers on the table in front of him. "We've read your proposal", he said, "and while we can see the advantages to you, I have to say", and here he waved a deprecatory hand over the papers, "that we cannot quite see what is in it for us". Brookes was unfazed by this opener, and in fact found it mildly encouraging. If Lynx could really see nothing in the proposal these four senior executives would not now be expending their time on this meeting. "Gentlemen", he said, "we are entering the age of the motor car. It's already arrived in the U.S., where everybody and his Uncle Chuck own's a car of one sort or another". The four wise men opposite sat unflinching and Brookes forged on. "It's now starting in Europe, and big companies like yours and small companies like mine have a few short years to make sure we're ready for the boom when it comes".

"You paint a rosy picture", said Standish, his tone betraying neither agreement nor disagreement, "how do you see this boom developing?"

"As Europe recovers", continued Brookes, "people, principally younger people, are going to want cars. Essentially your company and mine will sell to the same demographic, but I'll sell them sports cars when they're single and you'll sell them sports saloons when they're married, and the best way for us both to gain access to this market is through motor sport".

"A programme for which", chimed in the accountant, "you wish us to pay while you risk nothing". Alan Francis fielded that one. "You say 'risk' as if we were suggesting that you undermine the very foundations of your business. Not a bit of it. For a company the size of Lynx the budget will be tiny, and the potential rewards out of all proportion to expenditure. It will be the best investment you'll ever make".

"How tiny is tiny?" asked Standish, and the accountant referred to his sheaf of papers, "one hundred and fifty thousand", he said, fixing the two men opposite with a gimlet-eyed stare over the top of his pince-nez. "Pounds", said Standish reflectively. "Pounds", said the accountant as if it was his money. The four wise men lapsed into silent contemplation and Brookes and Francis glanced at each other. Francis raised his eyebrows and nodded in the direction of the Lynx directors. "In addition", said Brookes, "we will ensure that you are the first in the market with a sports saloon".

"How do you propose to do that?" asked Standish.

"I've had a look at the Monaco", said Brookes, "it's not bad, but it's a bit stodgy". Francis glanced at the ceiling, and the Lynx Chief Designer and Chief Engineer looked decidedly miffed. "You could do better?" asked Standish. "What I can do", said Brookes, "is introduce the car, and Lynx, to a whole new market. Without the need for a complete redesign I will give you some ideas for transforming the handling and road holding, and Alan here will design a few modifications for the standard engine to give it a bit of zip, then hey presto you have a new car. We could call it the Pegasus-Monaco, or something like that, and we would all benefit. Lynx has a name for building good quality saloons; Pegasus has a name for building good quality sports cars, as you will see if you read any of the road tests that are around". Ryan opened his mouth to speak but Standish got in first, "I have read them", he said, turning to Alan Francis. "And what do you expect to get from this Mr Francis?" he asked. The engineer paused to order his thoughts before replying. "As you see from our proposal, with your financial backing I can build a race winning engine based on the Monaco block, I've done a lot of the design work already. Basically the engine will be a three litre double-four valve 90 degree V8. We might call it the Grove-Lynx V8, or something along those lines, and with that engine in motor sport, and a lot of publicity around our joint Monaco road car project, we all three stand to benefit massively". Standish leaned back in his chair and for a moment there was contemplative silence, however nature abhors a vacuum and Ryan seized his chance. "You both seem to be ignoring the world situation", he said, "our problems with Egypt grow worse daily, we might yet have war over Suez with all that implies for oil supplies".

"We won't", replied Brookes confidently, and Standish leaned forward. "You seem very sure", he said, "why?"

"Because Eden is the diplomat's diplomat, quite apart from which, he was Foreign Secretary in Churchill's Cabinet through six years of war, he's as sick of all that as the rest of us, he won't let it get that far". Brookes paused briefly before continuing, "besides", he said reflectively, "even if the worst does come to the worst, if you intend to wait around for a period of world calm when everything in the garden is lovely", and here he looked Standish in the eye, "you will be marking time while your competitors forge ahead and take your markets away from you". Alan Francis winced and Sir Charles Standish leaned back to have a hushed discussion with his co-directors, on conclusion of which he turned back to his visitors with a smile that was almost warm. "I've seen you before Mr Brookes", he said. "Oh?" replied the Pegasus director, trying without success to remember the occasion, "where?" "I have seen you race at Donington, and at Silverstone, you were pretty good. A very distinctive helmet you had, claret coloured with a winged Pegasus logo. Were you perhaps in the Parachute Regiment?"

"No", Sir Charles", replied Brookes, "that was my brother, he was killed at Arnhem".

"Ah, I'm sorry".

"Me too, I miss him a lot, but we have to move on. I was in the Fleet Air Arm myself, a pilot, I flew Seafires". Standish's chubby face broke into a smile, "ah yes", he said, "the Navy's version of the Spitfire, so that's where the name for your sports car came from. I did wonder".

"Well gentlemen", asked Brookes, keen to move the meeting on, "what do you think? Can we do business?" Francis glanced at the four wise men and tried to read their minds - the Accountant showed nothing and Standish looked thoughtful. The engineer and the designer he was sure would argue against, they would want to save face by promising that they could do everything that was required themselves. This, he thought, is going to be touch-and-go, and then slowly the accountant turned to Standish and raised his eyebrows in unspoken question. A smile flicked across The Chairman's face and he stood, "we will discuss your proposal further and let you know as soon as we can", he said, and at this everybody stood and Brookes and Francis shook hands with their hosts. As the visitors were leaving the boardroom, Brookes turned back. "I told my father about this meeting, Sir Charles", he said, "and he told me he'd seen you before".

"Oh?" replied Standish, curious, "where?" Brookes face broke into a broad grin, "he saw you race at Brooklands back in the twenties. He says you were pretty good". Standish flushed, "oh, yes, well, I did a lap or two I suppose", he mumbled, and his companions looked at him in surprise. "You're too modest", said Brookes, and the two visitors turned on their heels and left.

As they walked back to the car Brookes asked Francis how he thought the meeting had gone and the engineer explained his feeling that the engineers would be against, but that Standish could well be for. The accountant he was not sure about. "I agree about the engineers", said Brookes, "I think we put their noses well out of joint. But the accountant was for us, did you see the look he gave Standish? I'm sure he was for. If your inside man is right and Lynx *do* have plans to get into motor racing he knows we can save them a lot of wasted time, and most importantly, wasted money". The two men reached the car and Brookes looked skywards at dark cloud formations drifting away to the west. The weather had cleared; a thaw was in progress and the carpet of snow turned to slush, hastened on the roads by the overnight work of gritting lorries. The two men chatted animatedly about the meeting as Brookes drove them back, and as he turned onto the A1 he accelerated away and the snarl of the performance engine under the bonnet rose as their speed increased. Traffic was light and Brookes allowed himself to have a little fun, approaching roundabouts by easing the car from the fast lane to the inside to even out the corner, double de-clutching down through the gears and roaring through the bends, holding the car on the optimum line by deftly balancing it between accelerator and steering, feeling what was happening on the road up through his spine, gently correcting the car with smooth movements of the wheel as it tried to break away in the glistening slush. "I like driving in the wet", he said, grinning boyishly. "Are you going to drive the racer?" asked Francis. "Me? At the Targa? Good God, no", responded Brookes, perhaps just a little too quickly, "I'd like to, but I'll have enough to do running the team. We'll hire professionals to do the driving. The race is over eight hours long so we'll need four of them for the two cars, with me maybe down as a reserve so that I can do a few test laps, see how she's handling".

"How will you pay for drivers?" asked Francis, "even if we get the Lynx deal that won't cover everything by a long shot".

"Well, I've dropped that particular hot potato in Mark Spall's lap…"

"Oh I bet he was delighted with that!" exclaimed Francis and again the infectious grin lit Brookes face. "Oh he'll wring his hands and worry about it", he said, "but Mark's got his head screwed on alright, I'd lay good odds he comes up with something".

Charlie Small was just that, small, and wiry and quick witted. Charlie worked for Pegasus, as did his mate, Freddie Kendal, and both had a wonderful way with cars. Both lads enjoyed the work but the pay wasn't great, and since both spent their weekends in London's East End in the cheerful pursuit of birds, booze, and fags, they arrived at the conclusion that what they needed was a sideline. So it was that in the Plough and Harrow in Leytonstone late one fateful Saturday night, topped up with mild and bitter and endeavouring to empty the little packet of salt into a bag of crisps, Charlie came up with the chimney sweep brainwave. It was perfect, he reasoned, with cold winters like the one in which they presently shivered, everybody had coal fires on the go and everybody needed their chimneys swept. Providentially, it turned out that Freddie's uncle Sid knew of a bloke called Alf who had been a chimney sweep before the war. Unfortunately Alf had not returned from Normandy, but Sid thought his widow might still have the brushes and possibly even the van. Of course the van hadn't turned a wheel for fifteen years or so, but that would not trouble mechanics of the calibre of Fred and Charlie.

The lads could not afford a car but managed to rescue a clapped out 1921 Triumph 550 cc motorcycle from a scrap dealer and coax it into life, and on the Sunday following Charlie's alcohol induced revelation they were puttering their smoky way to Ilford, where lived Glynis, widow of the former chimney sweep Alf.

The house was a tidy little semi on a corner of The Drive, with a neat garden at the front, and around to one side a large gate leading to the rear of the property. The lads parked the bike at the kerb outside and got off. Charlie pulled down his cloth cap, removed the stub of a cigarette from his mouth, dropped it on the pavement and stubbed it out with a booted foot. "Now listen", he said, "let me do the talkin', OK?"

"OK", agreed Freddie, more than happy to let Charlie do the talking. The two walked along a path between neat rows of flower beds and rose bushes to the front door, and Charlie knocked. The door opened, and granted Glynis was not in the first flush of youth, but she evidently looked after herself and was quite attractive in her own way... Charlie blinked and pulled his thoughts back to the matter in hand. "Charlie Small", he said by way of introduction, "an' Freddie Kendal, I think his uncle Sid spoke to you about..."

"Oh yes", she said, "the chimney sweeping stuff, come in, come in". They stepped into the hallway and Freddie closed the door behind them. Following Glynis through her neatly kept house they came out into the back yard, for yard it was, not a garden, and in the yard, covered in a tarpaulin, stood the van. "It's under there", she said. "Can we take the tarp off", asked Charlie, and she agreed.

The lads set to removing the tarpaulin and all the while Glynis stood by the back door watching. "Shame about your old man", said Charlie, by way of conversation. "I know", she replied, "he was a good bloke, but it's twelve years now, seems like a lifetime ago". Finally the tarpaulin slipped off to reveal a 1931 side valve Morris Minor van and on the face of it not in too bad condition, considering. "The other stuff's inside", she said from the doorway, "here's the keys". She held out her hand, the bunch of keys dangling from them. Charlie stepped over to get them, and she looked at him and he looked at her. It has to be said that Charlie was a bit of a ladies man, especially one bit, and was not slow on the uptake in that direction so he took the keys and tossed them to Freddie. "Give 'er a look over", he said, winked, and turned to follow Glynis back into the house. Freddie caught the keys, his glance flicked heavenwards, and he turned to open the back doors. Inside were brushes, rods, and all the paraphernalia they would need. Walking around to the driver's door, he opened it and looked inside, taking in the fifteen years of dust that hung in the atmosphere and covered the interior in a grey carpet. Finally he opened one side of the gullwing bonnet, checked the oil, pumped the carburettor and spent time giving the motor a good look over. "How is it?" asked Charlie, from behind him. Freddie turned and smiled, "deader'n Hitler", he said, taking in his companion's ruffled hair and generally flushed appearance, "how's the lady of the house?" Charlie glanced over his shoulder, "alive and bloody kicking", he said, "now", he continued, stepping to the van, "can we get this thing going?"

"Oh, I suppose so", mused Freddie, confident in their ability to fix anything mechanical, "depends what she wants for it". Charlie wrinkled his nose, "she says we can use it, just give her a few bob now and then from what we make".

"Plus a visit or two from Rudolf Valentino here", said Freddie and Charlie snatched the cap from his pocket and flicked Freddie across the ear with it.

3

"Sponsorship", said Mark Spall, leaning back in the chair in his office, quietly pleased with himself. "We raise money from sponsorship".

"You mean advertising on the cars?" asked Mike Brookes, unenthusiastically. "Possibly", confirmed Spall, "but not necessarily. You do see it sometimes in The States, but as yet rarely in Europe. The point is that the Targa Florio gets terrific coverage all over Europe; it's on T.V., in cinema newsreels, sports and national daily papers, it has its own massive market just waiting to be tapped."

"Have you contacted anybody yet?"

"No, Mike, I was waiting to discuss it with you first. What do you think?"

"I think it could work, but stay away from advertising on the cars if you possibly can. OK look, get on it right away; see who's interested - and there's something else you can use to reel them in, I want us to have a stand at the Motor Show this year..."

"Mike, that's an expensive business, let's not get ahead of ourselves here..."

"It's an expensive business if the stand is in with the other car manufacturers, but the Swift is marketed as a kit car, so we'll have a stand in the components section where it's much cheaper..."

"Crafty bastard", said Spall. "Thank you for that vote of confidence", smiled Brookes. "I'll also have a word with Alan Francis; see if he can throw something into the pot. It makes sense for us to have a joint stand with Grove Engineering". Brookes paced backwards and forwards across the small office and ran a hand through his hair. "Now look", he continued animatedly, "when we set up the stand, in addition to the Swift we'll also have a mock-up of the race car, so you can tell advertisers that if they get a move on they can have their logos on the car and reclining in the full glare of the world's media at the London Motor Show". Brookes stopped pacing and the two men looked at each other, suddenly aware that the project might actually get off the ground. Of course neither car nor engine existed as yet, and there was still the question of tyres, and..."Heard anything from Lynx?" asked Spall, expressing the foremost thought in both their minds. "Not yet", Brookes replied, "It's just over a week now. I'll give them a bit longer, then I'll call Standish".

Two days later Brookes leaned back in his chair in the office and put his feet up on the desk. It was late, the factory was dark, and the light from the lamp on his desk splashed across the day's paperwork. It had been a hell of a day in which both he and Mark Spall found themselves obliged to spend valuable time smoothing the ruffled feathers of the damn bank manager, once more in headless chicken mode concerning the overdraft. Having at last pacified the man Mark Spall rushed off to meet the blonde bombshell and take her to see this season's theatrical hit, Agatha Christie's *The Mousetrap,* in London, and Brookes picked up the glass, sipped the whisky and felt the knot of nerves at the back of his neck relax a little. Brookes replaced the glass on the desk and stood. He decided to have one more look before leaving for home, and stepping out of the office proceeded along the walkway, down the steel steps and switched on a light. The brittle glow from the fluorescent tube revealed Seafires in various stages of construction, but where once had languished a large unused area at the rear of the factory, now there stood a newly erected floor to ceiling partition. Brookes walked to the partition, opened a door, stepped through and switched on the light. The familiar fluorescent glow splashed around the large sectioned off area, but this time to reveal the skeleton of a race car. Skeleton was an appropriate word for the spaceframe, which comprised high grade steel tubing in triangulated sections welded together for maximum strength and rigidity, both being essential requirements, strength to take on the notorious mountain section of the car-breaking Targa circuit and rigidity to give the car excellent handling characteristics. Flexing of the chassis would ruin the car's road holding and make it practically un-drivable for competition purposes. A third essential to arise from the spaceframe design was weight saving, for the complete skeleton weighed in at no more than 42 lbs. This was the purest form of the spaceframe design that Brookes could come up with, and it did have one significant drawback – accessibility, or to be precise, lack of it! Getting at the engine would be a nightmare should they need to work on it during a race but Brookes decided that this pinnacle of the design was necessary for the Targa. He could always work on a modified version for the less demanding purpose built race tracks that made up much of the World Sports Car Championship. Slowly he walked around the finished frame, visualising the divided front axle and his own modification of a De Dion axle at the rear to reduce wheel spin. Pegasus did not have the necessary equipment or engineers to build the frames themselves, so the work was sub-contracted, but Brookes was well pleased the with result, the chassis appearing to conform to all his specifications.

Gazing at the car, his mind switched into over-drive, turning over a tumbling landslide of innovations. He calculated that with engine, running gear and body panels in place, the complete car should not tip the scales at more than 11 hundredweight, assuming that Alan Francis' calculations as to the final weight of the three-litre power plant were correct. Then through the lightning flashes of his own ideas and dreams he slowly became aware of the distant ringing of a telephone in his office. That would be Nicola wondering where he was, and coming reluctantly back down to earth he switched out the light, fished in a pocket for his keys, closed the door behind him and sprinted across the workshop and up the stairs to the office. Picking up the telephone he was for a fraction of a second nonplussed by the fact that it was a male voice at the other end. "Mr Brookes", it said, "Charles Standish here".

"Sir Charles", Brookes replied, attempting to sound calm while suddenly tense with expectation, "what can I do for you?"

"Still working I see, Mr. Brookes. I telephoned your home number first; a charming young lady told me you were still at the factory".

"Ah yes, that would be Nicola, my fiancé". A pause at the other end of the line seemed to Brookes to last for hours, and then Standish spoke again. "Mr Brookes, I have to be in London for a few days, would it be possible for us to meet?"

"Certainly", said Brookes, his mind racing over the possibilities almost as fast as his heart rate, "where did you have in mind?"

"I will be staying at The Dorchester, could you meet me there the day after tomorrow at, say, seven pm?"

"I'll be there, Sir Charles".

"Good, good, I look forward to it", replied Standish as if he meant it and he hung up. With his brain working overtime on the prospects for the meeting Brookes locked the office, walked along the gangway and down the steps, pulled closed first one and then the other of the large, corrugated, factory doors, and carefully locked them. He had not until recently been particularly security conscious, especially out here in the wilds of Essex, but was aware that industrial espionage was not unknown in the motor industry, and that details of the new car would be marketable properties.

The day after tomorrow took its time but eventually arrived and found London enveloped in one of those pea-souper smogs for which it was justly famous. Brookes decided to drive the car as far as Ilford and go into 'The Smoke' by train. On hearing of the meeting both Mark Spall and Alan Francis advised him to keep calm until he heard what Standish had to say, but despite this good advice, with his nerves already in shreds, the seemingly endless journey to London as the train huffed and puffed its own smoky contribution to the gloom outside, was close to driving him to distraction. It seemed to Brookes that fate conspired to ensure that nothing could take his thoughts from the potentially make-or-break meeting that he was about to have. Outside the carriage fog blanketed any potential view in swirling dirty grey, relieved only by the occasional bright smoky glow from a trackside light, and at this time in the evening most travellers were on their way home from London, ensuring that any train going in the opposite direction would be practically deserted, he being the only occupant of the compartment in which he sat.

On arrival in London Brookes' frustration mounted as taxis were scarcer than horse feathers due to the weather and he wasted much time chasing one after the other, until finally he found a ride and climbed aboard. Still his frustration knew no end as the taxi crawled bumper to bumper through fog bound traffic, until finally he arrived at Park Lane and the entrance to the hotel. Brookes glanced at his watch as he paid the taxi fare and bounded up the steps to the entrance. He was late.

Striding quickly up the steps and pushing through the throng of people in the foyer on their way to the theatre or the cinema, or going to dinner, he arrived at reception, introduced himself and asked where he might find Sir Charles Standish. Directed to The Dorchester Bar, he made his way there and upon entering was relieved to find that it was early evening quiet. Glancing around he located Standish, who spotted him at the same time and waved him over. Arriving at last, a little breathless, with his heart beating like a hammer, and aware that this was not the best preparation for an important meeting, Brookes tried to appear calm, apologised for being late, and sat at the table. Standish was charm itself, asked what Brookes would like to drink and ordered Scotch and Canada Dry on the rocks for his guest and gin and tonic for himself. "So, Mr Brookes", said Standish as Brookes took a sip of the Scotch, "that was your fiancé that I spoke to the other night".
"Nicola, yes".
"How long have you been engaged?"

"Oh, a little over a year now", responded Brookes and Standish grimaced comically, "long time", he said, "long time, the lady will be getting restless". Brookes smiled, relaxed a little by the Scotch and his companion's easy manner. "Well", he said, "her mother certainly is!"

"Do you have any plans for naming the day?" asked Standish and Brookes pondered for a moment. "Well to tell you the truth", he said at length, "I have, but I haven't mentioned it to anybody yet".

"Do tell", Standish whispered conspiratorially. "Well, I have always maintained with Nicola that I would name the day when the business was set fair and well on its way, so I have decided that I will ask her when a Pegasus car wins next year's Targa Florio". Standish took a cigar case from his jacket pocket, offered them to his companion, who refused, took one for himself and enjoyed the leisurely ritual of clipping and lighting it. "Surely", he said finally, through a cloud of expensive cigar smoke, "you mean when a Pegasus *Lynx* wins the '57 Targa Florio?" Caught with the tumbler of whisky part way to his lips, Brookes blinked and wondered if he had heard right. "You mean you'll do it!?" He exclaimed, plonking the glass down on the table and splashing Scotch. "Well", said Standish, smiling, "we're not there yet, but I have hopes. You must bear in mind", he continued, "that Lynx is a very old established company which has never engaged in anything as brash and loud as motor racing, it is taking my colleagues some time to come to a final decision, but in the meantime they have authorised me to put an offer to you."

"And that is?" Brookes asked as Standish took a sip from his drink and puffed on the cigar. "Your proposal", the Lynx Chairman said, "was based upon a two car team, for which you say you would need four complete engines plus a test bed prototype. Our proposal would be based on a singleton entry, one complete engine and a test bed prototype. We would inject seventy five thousand pounds into the project and would take a share in Pegasus of say 20 percent. If we are successful next year we can talk about an increased budget for the following year. What do you say?" Standish sat back and watched his companion carefully. For his part, Brookes was tempted. This was not the deal he wanted but it would mean that they could go motor racing. He sipped the whisky and took a deep breath. "No", he said flatly, "the budget's too tight and cutting the team down is false economy. With two cars we *more* than double the chance of a good result at the Targa, and with a bit of luck we could even win," he said confidently, "additionally I am not happy about Lynx taking a share in Pegasus, although if necessary I might agree to a non-executive director appointed by the company to keep an eye on their investment". Standish smiled, "good", he said, "I hoped you'd say that. As I said Lynx have never contemplated anything like motor sport before, and Archie Rhead, our Chief Accountant, who you met at our meeting, argued against it from the start, but due in part to the timely arrival of your proposal we have now decided to take the plunge. Faced with a fait accompli Archie saw how a tie up with you and Alan Francis could save us a lot of time *and* money, but in true accountant's fashion he is still trying to pare expenditure on what he considers to be a highly speculative venture down to the bone". Brookes opened his mouth to speak, but Standish leaned forward and continued. "Now", he said animatedly, "If you will give me a little more time before approaching anyone else, I think I can put this deal together pretty much as you originally suggested. What do you say? Will you give me another week or so?" Brookes was nonplussed. This meeting was turning out to be something of a rollercoaster but he was quietly pleased to hear that Standish feared he might go elsewhere, which he had in fact not as yet considered. Affecting deep concentration, Brookes finally agreed to the extra week. "Good!" exclaimed the older man, "now let's have another drink!" With the arrival of the second drink, and a little more relaxed, Brookes asked what had tempted Lynx to consider entering motor racing in the first place. "Well that's one of those interesting coincidences on which events often turn", replied Standish. "We could not help but notice the huge publicity generated in Britain and all over Europe when Stirling Moss and Tony Brooks won the Targa last year for Mercedes, and while we were mulling that over, your proposal offering to enter a team in the 'fifty-seven Targa using Lynx engines plonked on my desk. Uncanny, eh?" His companion agreed and the two men chatted about cars and motor racing and the ups and downs of world affairs, until Standish finished his cigar and stubbed it out in the ashtray on the table. "Now", he said, glancing at his watch, "my good lady wife is waiting patiently for me to take her to the theatre, but before I go there is one more important item to clarify and that is tyres, have you done anything about tyres for the race car?"

"Not yet", replied Brookes a little ruefully, "it's next on my list of priorities after getting an engine".

"Were you aware that Shoji Takamura is due in London shortly?"

"Takamura? Of JTC? No, but they don't make a race tyre, and anyway they have practically no market penetration outside the Far East". Standish finished his drink. "Exactly so", he said, "the word is that Takamura wants to expand his Japan Tyre Company into Europe in a big way and sees motor racing as a central element for a major advertising campaign that he will be putting together. My understanding is that while here he will visit John Cooper, Brabham, and Colin Chapman at Lotus, to see about tyre contracts for their competition cars, evidently he has not considered Pegasus as he thinks that you have no motor racing ambitions".

"Evidently", replied Brookes pensively, "but *(A)* how do I get to him? and *(B)* will his tyres be any good? We are going to have enough fresh-out-of-the-box components for this project as it is, I was rather hoping that the bit that actually makes contact with the road would have a proven pedigree!" Standish laughed out loud, "well", he said, "If you have the budget that's fine, if not, you could do worse than talk to Takamura, JTC are a major force in the Far East and are not short of cash. If Takamura's as keen as rumour says he is, you might get an attractive package from him, and remember, those other companies he is going to see all have established suppliers; they are unlikely to want to make a move to a new tyre until they see if it performs". Brookes let out a long speculative breath, "ok", he said finally, "how do I contact him?"

"We have dealings with JTC in the Far East, let me set up a meeting for you, it will give you extra gravitas if he thinks you have the ear of Lynx".

"I'm very grateful", Brookes said genuinely, "I'd appreciate that".

"I want this thing to work as well, Mr Brookes", replied Standish with equal sincerity, "I'll be in touch".

At the Brookes home Nicola considered the problem; her glasses perched fetchingly on the end of her pert nose. "I think", she said finally, "that rather than having one contract covering all aspects of the arrangement, it would be far less complicated if Pegasus and Grove Engineering had a contract between them, detailing their areas of cooperation, and each company had a separate contract with Lynx."

"Assuming Standish comes up trumps", said Alan Francis, taking a drink from one of the newly fashionable canned lager's that Brookes kept in his 'fridge. "I don't think he would have said he could do it unless he was fairly sure of his ground", replied Brookes, "and it makes sense for us to be prepared". Outside the day dissolved into winter dusk and Brookes turned away from the window to the coal-fire warmth of their dining room. Nicola sat at the dining room table, the remains of their evening meal pushed to one side and the tabletop now littered with specifications, legal documents and notes. "If Lynx do go for this", continued Francis, "space will be a problem. I don't have enough room at the railway arches to build and develop the engine".

"Well, we have bags of room in the hangars; part of our contract could be for Grove to take space there. It makes sense for the chassis and engine to be developed in close proximity in any event".

"But if I'm out in Essex what happens to my own business?" asked Francis, "I will need to take on staff for the new project anyway, but on that basis I would need extra bodies for the arches as well". Brookes pondered the problem, and Nicola chimed in. "Mike, perhaps you could loan him one or two of your engineers, you could share their salaries between you".

"That might work", agreed Brookes, "Charlie Small is a bright lad and a good mechanic, him and that mate of his, Freddie Kendal. What d'you think Alan?"

"Yes that might work, I know both those lads of yours, we could put it to them, see what they say?"

The lads to whom Alan Francis referred were at that moment entering upon this latest in a long line of schemes to augment their wages - knelt in front of a fireplace a short distance from the Brookes residence. Freddie Kendal sniffed. "Well", he said, "the brush is in the chimney, that shield thing is over the fireplace, now what?"

"We just keep screwing on rods and pushing the brush farther up the chimney", Charlie opined confidently, "we'll know when the brush comes out the top because there won't be any resistance". At the bottom of each rod was fixed a brass ball joint to which the next rod was attached, enabling the brush to follow the contours of the chimney as it made its way onwards and upwards. Freddie duly picked up a rod, screwed it to the end of the rod protruding from the shield and together they pushed. "Bloody hell", gasped Charlie, "this is hard work". Many rods and much heaving later, the two heavily perspiring sweeps called a halt. "That brush should be out by now", gasped Charlie. "Not according to all the trouble we're havin' pushing the bugger", replied his companion "must be a long bloody chimney, that's all I can say".

"Freddie, lad" said Charlie patiently, "we've nearly run out of rods and this is a bleedin' bungalow! Now, you're nearest the door, just pop outside and see what you can see." Freddie got wearily to his feet, stepped out into the hallway, opened the front door and the brush hit him full in the face. Knocked back against the wall a startled chimney sweep let out a yell and fell to the floor with a thump. Arriving home from a hard day's work, hands in the pockets of his working clothes, a middle aged man stepped past the dangling brush and into the hallway. "Think you've got enough rods on there, son?" he asked, nonchalantly. "Ah", quoted the soot-faced Freddie in embarrassment, "Mr. Chitty, you're home".

"I am", replied the man, surveying his domain, "my missus here?" At that moment Mrs Chitty rushed from the kitchen and Charlie raced out of the lounge, chorusing "what's all the noise?" in unison. "Dinner ready?" asked Mr Chitty of his wife, stepping over the recumbent Freddie and past his spouse, hands still in pockets. "Perhaps he's got a car needs fixing?" asked Freddie of no-one in particular.

It would have to happen on a Monday-bloody-morning, he thought irritably as he pedalled his way onward. If they had a big bundle of letters or some packets or something useful like that he could have given it all to the van driver to bring out here, but no, one letter, one bloody letter, so here he was at the end of his duty having to pedal all the way out to this bloody airfield, and it was raining stair rods, water splashing off his rubberised cape, dripping down the back of his neck and from the peak of his cap onto his nose. The postman pulled his bike to a halt at the wrought iron gates, dismounted, pushed it up to the factory and leaned it against the wall. "Mr Brookes here?" he called. Charlie Small's head popped up from the engine of a Seafire on which he worked, "upstairs, mate", he said, "in the office". 'Perfect' thought the Postman, bloody stairs now, and trudging up the stairs and along the walkway he arrived finally at the office door and knocked. Asked to enter, he opened the door and stepped through.

"Mr Brookes?" he asked, and on being given an affirmative reply, pulled an envelope from the pouch under his cape, "letter to sign for", he said, handing both letter and receipt slip across the desk. Having obtained his signature, the Postman trudged wearily back down the stairs, mounted his trusty steed and pedalled for the nearest pub.

Back in the office Mike Brookes cradled the letter in his hands, his mouth suddenly dry. The letter was addressed to him and bore the Lynx Motor Company logo in the top left hand corner. Slowly Brookes reached out a hand for the letter opener, slid it under the flap and slit the envelope open. Carefully removing the letter, he took a deep breath, unfolded it, read it, blinked, read it again and letting out an ecstatic whoop leapt from his chair and yanked open the interconnecting door to the next office. "They've gone for it!" he yelled at the startled Mark Spall, "they've agreed!" he said, tossing the letter on Spall's desk. Spall picked it up, read and re-read it. "Bloody hell", he gasped in amazement, "you got pretty much what you wanted". He smiled. "Looks like we're going motor racing!" he said. "Too bloody right!" exclaimed Brookes, "now Mark, how are you getting along with sponsorship and the Motor Show?"
"I have meetings this week with potential sponsors, and on Thursday I'm in London sorting out our stand for the Show".
"Good man! Best not name Lynx to the sponsors until we get serious interest, for the time being just say we have an engine deal with a major manufacturer, OK?"
"OK". Behind Brookes the telephone in his office rang and he hurried to pick it up. "Hello!" he barked, and at the other end of the line a near hysterical Alan Francis gabbled

41

on about a letter he had just received from Lynx. Mike Brookes took a deep breath. "I know", he said, calming down, "I got the same letter; I suppose we'd better start getting our act together hadn't we?"

4.

A leisurely drive south from Palermo, Sicily's capital city and infamous Mafia stronghold, the coast road passes through Bagheria, long-time playground for the Sicilian aristocracy and home to many of the most spectacular villas in Europe. Most had now passed from the landed gentry to rich merchant families, but one remained, the home of Don Pietro de Sevilla y Cordoba, 10th Prince of Aspra, a peer of the realm with a family blood line traceable back to the Spanish nobility of the 15th century. Don Pietro's ancestors prided themselves on their knowledge of fine horses, racing magnificent Arab stallions that they obtained from the Moors. For the current incumbent of the Villa Cordoba, however, the passion was not for horses, but horse power.

When it became apparent that a rich, languid, existence was no longer possible merely by the good fortune of being born into the aristocracy, the Cordoba family had the 'common' (they would have recoiled at the word!) sense to use its substantial fortune to develop commercial interests. Commerce being looked down upon by their aristocratic peers the House of Cordoba fell out of favour with the Spanish court and moved lock stock and barrel to Sicily, where their interests flourished while their aristocratic contemporaries fell one by one into oblivion.

The Cordoba family now operated a vast commercial empire based on clothing, mass market but fashionable, elegant, and making full use of the world-famous Italian flair for design. All this enabled Don Pietro to indulge his passion for racing cars by owning one of the most successful post-war racing teams in Europe, using his seemingly limitless wealth to purchase the most competitive cars of the day for his team - Maseratis, Alfas,

Lancias, Ferraris, and one season even Mercedes, although he held a strong personal preference for the dramatic, romantic, Italian machines. Bright cherry-red Scuderia Cordoba cars had at one time or another during the past ten years won every major motor race around the world. Every major motor race, this is, except one, the sheer magic of which had drawn this aristocratic Sicilian nobleman into motor racing in the first place, the race virtually on Don Pietro's doorstep, the Targa Florio.

Even at this early hour in the morning the day was already warm. Don Pietro Cordoba, dressed casually in open necked shirt and slacks, strolled across the magnificent ballroom of the villa, with its mirrored tiles adorning the ceiling, and stood on the balcony that looked out across the deep turquoise blue Mediterranean. Idly he smoked a cigarette, glancing toward the main gate at the sound of a car drawing to a halt outside. Crowning the magnificent stone portico that housed the gate stood a group of grotesque stone statues, which, legend said, were placed there on the orders of the 6th Prince, as freakish representations of his wife's lovers. Judging by the number of similar statues dotted around the villa's capacious grounds she must have been a lady of prodigious appetite!

Don Pietro watched as a footman hurried to the gate and opened it to allow a silver Lancia to enter and approach the residence. Moments later he heard the soft deferential footsteps as a servant approached across the ballroom. "Don Pietro", the man breathed quietly, "Signor Castellotti has arrived". Instructed to show the visitor in, the servant withdrew to be replaced by the echo of shoes approaching across the marbled floor. "Don Pietro", their wearer began apologetically from behind The Don, "what can I say?" An experienced team manager, Salvatore Castellotti managed Scuderia Cordoba and truly hated being summoned to the villa, which, it seemed to him, only happened when there were bad results. Good results were expected and so were apparently not worthy of comment.

"What happened this time?" asked the nobleman without turning. Castellotti took a deep breath, "we were leading comfortably with the Maserati", he began, attempting to appear upbeat, but his voice trailed away to the bad news, "but the car developed a leak in one of the lateral fuel tanks and had to keep returning to the pits for refuelling. It put us down to third place at the finish".

"So, once again", replied Don Pietro, his voice icy calm, "we fail to win the Targa. Always there is something. There is an accident, or the car breaks, or we have the wrong driver, always there is something! Well I tell you Signor Castellotti, we will not fail again. Do you hear me! Now, the remainder of this season, and next season up to the Targa in June will be considered as mere preparation for that race. Do what you have to do, consider expense no object, but by June next year I want a team in place that will bring me the Targa!" The unfortunate Castellotti had delivered many victories for the Don in his three years as team manager, but knew very well his patron's obsession with the Sicilian race and so mumbled his agreement. Don Pietro made an impatient, dismissive motion with his hand, but as the chastened team manager turned to leave, the nobleman spoke again. "Signor Castellotti, what of Nalbandian?" Castellotti stopped and turned back to his employer. "Jorge Nalbandian is an exceptionally talented young driver. It is said that he may even be better than Fangio".

"He drives for Ferrari does he not?"

"He is committed to the Ferrari Grand Prix team for the current year and for next year, Don Pietro".

"I want him to drive for me in the Targa, see what can be arranged". Castellotti wiped a hand across his perspiring brow. "That might be difficult, Don Pietro, with both the French and British Grand Prix traditionally run in close proximity to the Targa, his Ferrari commitments will take priority, and Ferrari may very well require him to drive in the Targa as well". Castellotti stared at his employer's back, awaiting a reply. "See what can be arranged", repeated the Don, "if necessary I will speak with him myself". The Don took a long draw on the cigarette and blew smoke upward into a cloudless azure blue sky. "What news of Pegasus?" he asked at last. "Rumours of a cooperation with Lynx continue", replied Castellotti, "it is said that an announcement will be made at the London Motor Show in the autumn. It is not presently known what type of race car is involved".

"Ah, these British *garagistes*", said Cordoba with a shrug, "they will never amount to anything, an engine from here, a gearbox from there, what do they hope to accomplish? You cannot build thoroughbred racing machines in such a manner."

"I am not so sure", replied Castellotti, who was prepared to contradict the Don on occasion, and felt that this was such an occasion, "the likes of Michael Brookes, John Cooper and Colin Chapman are all superb engineers; they know their business and the cars they build will be competitive. We have already seen how Chapman has transformed the Vanwall Grand Prix car". Again the long draw on the cigarette before Cordoba spoke, "very well", he said at last, "it will do no harm to discover what Pegasus are up to". With a wave of an aristocratic hand the interview was concluded and this time Castellotti made his grateful escape.

Jorge Nalbandian, the Argentinean driver of whom Don Pietro spoke, had been a spectator at this year's Targa and decided to remain in Sicily for a few days before going on to France to drive in the French Grand Prix in early July. He knew the Targa well by repute and wanted very much to drive in this most challenging of all races with its twisting mountain section and the exhilarating 6km arrow straight but narrow road along the coast, taken at speeds of 175mph or more. However, plead though he might for his chance, Commendatore Ferrari insisted that he was not yet ready; more experience would be required before tackling a race like the Targa. This would be no two hour Grand Prix sprint on a purpose built track – he would have to drive for three to four hours at a stretch over tortuous public roads with 832 bends and corners for every 72 kilometre lap. The Commendatore then held out a hand and tapped it. 'Your hand' he said, 'even with gloves, would be red raw with blisters from the gear changing required'. He shrugged, 'perhaps next year', he said.

Coming as he did from one of the wealthiest land-owning families in Argentina, Jorge Nalbandian was not used to being denied anything that he desired and Ferrari's refusal ruffled his Latin pride. Coincidentally, like Don Pietro, he now stood on a balcony overlooking the Mediterranean, this particular balcony being located at the expensive, exclusive hotel at which he stayed. He turned

47

back to the bedroom, the bed, and the girl. She was very beautiful, but so were they all, a different one for each race. He stepped back into the room and removed the towel from his lean, tanned, midriff. "Now", he said, "where were we?" and she smiled.

5.

'Typical' thought Mike Brookes, 'whenever things were going to plan you could always trust a bunch of politicians to balls it up!' He read the newspaper article again. The US/British spat with Nasser's Egypt had started to boil, and there was much name calling and petulant stamping of feet. 'To bloody hell with all politicians' thought Brookes, but at that moment a faint but distinctive roar cut through his mental tirade and he leapt to his feet and dashed out of his office, narrowly missing Mark Spall as he emerged from his own office, and the two men ran along the walkway and down the steps. Alan Francis had installed his new engine development department in what had been the airfield maintenance block, a short distance from the hangars that Pegasus occupied. Now extensively rebuilt and re-equipped using Lynx funds, it was from this block that the sound that caught Brooke's and Spall's attention emanated and it was to there that they ran pell mell. Peering in through a window in the block they rapped on the window, but inside Alan Francis and several engineers, all wearing ear protectors and poring over a control panel, took no notice. Brookes banged, thumped, and yelled in impatience until finally one of the group looked up and spotted them. Tapping Francis on an arm he pointed at the window, and looking over his shoulder Francis turned a switch and the noise abated. The door was opened from inside and Brookes recognised Harold Cooper, Lynx Chief Engineer and the car company's representative overseeing their investment. "Bloody marvellous' gasped Cooper as Brookes and Spall pushed past him, "bloody marvellous" he said again. "Well!?" asked Brookes impatiently as Francis smiled knowingly, "don't just stand there bloody grinning", Brookes continued, "how did the test go?" Alan

Francis turned back to the control panel, beyond which a glass panel was set into a wall. Beyond the panel, in the dynamometer cell, the gleaming new Grove Lynx V8 sat, silent now on its test bed. Turning back Francis leaned nonchalantly on the control panel while Brookes with difficulty resisted an impulse to throttle him. "Over three hundred horsepower", said Francis finally, "we'll get over three hundred horses in race trim, confirmed same as the last test". Brookes yelled with delight and punched the air in exultation. "With the spaceframe that means a power to weight ratio of less than two kilos per horsepower. Bloody hell - that's streets better than Ferrari or anybody else has managed!"

"How's the chassis coming along?" asked Francis. "Nearly there", replied Brookes excitedly, "just a few bits and pieces to tinker with".

"Are you sure the chassis will handle the power?" asked the engineer. "Sure, sure," replied Brookes with a dismissive wave of a hand. "Which just leaves the tyres", interjected Spall, and Brookes came back to earth with a bump. "Yes", he said, "I've been trying everywhere but the damn tyre companies are either fully committed and can't or won't increase their production run, or they're too expensive".

"What about JTC?" asked Spall, and Brookes' glance flicked to the ceiling and back in exasperation. "Takamura's cancelled his trip to Europe twice now..."

"Bastard Japs" muttered Francis, "can't trust 'em and we shouldn't be doing business with them."

""We're not - yet", countered Brookes, "and anyway the war's finished Alan, we all have to get over it. As for Takamura's movements, apparently he's now due here next month. I'll give Standish a call, see what's going on".

He looked over his shoulder, "have you heard anything, Harold?" he asked the Lynx director. "Not a thing", replied Cooper, "but I'm sure Sir Charles will do all he can". Before leaving Brookes turned back to Alan Francis, "how are those two boyos of mine getting on down at your lockup?" he asked. Francis smiled, "Fred and Charlie are having the time of their life in the big city", he said, "chasing everything that sashays past in a skirt".
"And their work?"
"First rate, you'd have heard from me long and loud if it wasn't, but they're both damn fine mechanics". Brookes waved a hand in acknowledgement and he and Spall left. Strolling back to their offices the two men chatted animatedly about the project. Spall had some interesting feedback from potential sponsors but Brookes, in addition to tyres, had four drivers to find.

Seated back at his desk Brookes folded the newspaper, and there was the note. Peter Snelgrove had telephoned and left a number for him to call. The name was famous and perhaps even infamous. Snelgrove drove for both Mercedes and Auto Union in the thirties when those two mighty companies were flag wavers for the Nazi regime. Undoubtedly he was a superb driver, winning races for both teams but after the war an unofficial blacklist ensured that his career nosedived and he had not driven competitively for years. Ironically his former employers, Mercedes and Auto Union, went from strength to strength after the war, but even they refused to take him on, unwilling to be reminded of unfortunate associations that they felt best remained in the past. Brookes wondered what he wanted, but suspected he knew, rumours of the co-operation with Lynx must have been on the bush telegraph for months now. The telephone rang to interrupt his thoughts and Jeanine told him that a journalist working for an Italian motoring magazine, a Miss Gina d'Alessandro, was on the line asking for an interview. "Put her on to Mark", Brookes replied, "he has a way with the ladies, he should be able to get us a good write-up". He hung up the handset, heard the telephone ring in the next office and heard Mark Spall answer. The Pegasus boss ran a hand through his hair, looked with despair at the jumble of papers on his desk, scooped them up and stacked them in one corner under the Ark Royal badged paperweight that he kept there for the purpose. 'Now', he thought, 'I have four drivers to find'.

Interested to discover from his father that Standish had a racing pedigree, Brookes discussed current prospects with the Lynx Chairman, who suggested Adrian Rawnsley-Bysh. Standish knew the family and had seen Adrian race, counting him worth a chance. Adrian came from a wealthy background, being heir to a brewing fortune, and, importantly from a financial perspective, the family might be persuaded to buy him a drive, injecting much-needed funds into the project. Brookes would have liked at least one recognised winner in the line-up but the likes of Moss, Fangio, von Trips, Hawthorn, and Peter Collins were all committed to established teams, as well as being out of his league financially. Among the younger drivers Nalbandian was very quick but likewise under contract, in his case to Ferrari. Abruptly Brookes came to a decision, stood and stepped to the interconnecting door to Spall's office. Opening it, he poked his head through. "How'd you get on with the journalist?" he asked. Spall looked up, "fine", he replied, "I've arranged to meet her in a couple of day's time. I have to say if she looks anything as gorgeous as she sounds on the 'phone it will be a meeting I shall very much enjoy!"

"Well be discreet, Mark, I don't want details of the car getting out with over a year still to go to the race."

"That's why I thought I'd meet her in London, no chance of her wandering around the factory".

"Alright, good, she can have a photo or two of the race car for her article if she wants, but don't go into engine performance or tell her about the spaceframe chassis, OK?"

"OK Mike, I'll be discretion itself".

"Make sure you are", said Brookes only half joking, "I know you when you get around a good looking skirt, your brains take up residence in your trousers".

"Bloody cheek!" exclaimed Spall, smiling broadly. "Now", continued Brookes, "the car is coming along well, so I've spoken to Ken Gregory at the B.R.S.C.C. and booked Brands Hatch, that new circuit of theirs in Kent, for two days next month so that we can have a private shakedown trial. We can see what needs attention and test a few drivers at the same time".

"Good idea", interjected Spall, as Brookes forged on, "now, Mark, we've taken a big bite out of the Lynx money and we badly need to sort out some sponsorship. How are you getting on? Any decent prospects?"

"Well yes, actually", replied Spall thoughtfully, "I got wind of the fact that Holland & Pendlebury..."

"...The department store chain...?"

"That's them", confirmed Spall, "I got wind that they were looking to sharpen up their image. They've been around since the 1930's and feel that they've become a bit stale in the public's perception, not dissimilar to Lynx as a matter of fact, so they will be bringing out a line of own manufacture smart casual clothes with which they hope to take the bright new youth market by storm". Brookes ran a hand through his hair, "so where do we come in?" he asked. "Well, I contacted them and I've had a couple of long chats with their Chief Marketing Executive. He says they will be using a new brand name for the clothing, *Palm Beach*..."

"...And they want to advertise on the cars...?"

"No, Mike, not as such, I know you weren't too keen on that so what I have discussed with them is renaming the team..."

"...Renaming *what!?*... "

"Hold your horses Mike; we enter the cars under the name *Team Palm Beach Pegasus Lynx.* That name would be the *only* mention on the cars, and would also appear on the entry list, in magazine articles etcetera. In addition they would want photo shoots, you know the sort of thing, gorgeous models draped over the cars..."

"...and I wonder who thought of *that*...?"

"...not me for a change, that came from H & P. They would want to use our cars in their product launch, possibly including movie footage for cinema ads. If we do well in the Targa they would certainly want to make maximum use of that for their own publicity. Lots of detail to work out but that's it in essence, what do you think?" Brookes scratched his head, "hmm", he murmured, "it has possibilities, I have to admit. How much would they put in?"

"Haven't discussed money with them yet", replied Spall, "I wanted to sound you out first, but I want to try for something fairly substantial. Leave it with me; I'll let you know how I get on".

"OK but don't scare them off, the more I think of that tie-up the more I like it – if we have just one sponsor to deal with it will be much less time consuming and complicated than if there are loads of them". Brookes turned away and then turned back. "By the way, isn't one of the big Italian teams sponsored by a clothing manufacturer?" Spall smiled, "Scuderia Cordoba", he replied, "is *owned* by a major Italian clothing manufacturer, that's what gave me the idea when I heard about the H & P move into clothing. The advertising potential of taking Cordoba on and beating them in a high profile international sports setting was mouth watering bait to use with Holland and Pendlebury".

"Bloody good work. Now, screw them for every penny you can get but *don't* lose them! I don't want to find that with you having given them the idea they then swan off and sponsor someone else. Reel them in and land them, OK?" Spall smiled and waved a hand in acknowledgement as Brookes returned to his office.

6

It was a long drive up to Lancashire, but Brookes did not hurry. Soon enough he parked the car outside the small semi-detached house in the Preston suburb. Nicola got out carrying a bag containing a few groceries and some of the recipient's favourite cakes, while Brookes picked up a bag containing a bottle or two of the recipient's favourite ale. Together they walked up the neat path and Brookes knocked on the door. Shortly movement was heard behind the door, which then swung open to reveal a bespectacled man in his seventies, grey hair and moustache, a little shorter than Brookes and leaning on a walking stick, a necessity following an accident when he managed a country pub pre-war. "Hi dad", said the younger man. Arthur Brookes smiled and the two shook hands warmly. "Come in, both of you", he said, the Lancashire accent still noticeable but modulated by having lived for many years in and around London, until his wife, Mike's mother, had passed away. As the visitors stepped into the house Nicola kissed the man on the cheek, "hello pops", she said affectionately. "Not got that idle son of mine to marry you yet?" was the response, accompanied by a wink and a merry twinkle in the older man's eyes. "I'm working on it", she said, while ahead of them the object of their stage whispers groaned, "don't start already, the both of you", he said resignedly. Arthur Brookes closed the door and turned back to the new arrivals, "in the lounge", he said, and Mike turned left into a small, neatly furnished room. On top of a well-stocked bookcase stood two framed photographs, one of himself, one of his elder brother George in full Para uniform, proudly displaying sergeant's stripes. Arthur followed his son into the room as Nicola

spoke from the hallway, "I'll put the groceries in the kitchen", she said, indicating the bag. "You should marry that girl", Arthur said, "she's bright *and* beautiful, what the hell are you waiting for, a commandment carved on a tablet of stone?" Sitting on a sofa his son put a finger to his lips, "I know, I intend to", he replied quietly, "I just want the business to be better established. If we can get a good result at the Targa, a win even..." and the older man pursed his lips. "Well, yes, I know", continued Mike, "that's a bit optimistic, but a podium place anyway, it will set us up and I'll marry Nicola like a shot". Arthur Brookes sat in an armchair, against which leaned the walking stick. "Well don't leave it too long", he said, "she won't wait forever". Straightening his right leg he leaned forward to massage the knee. "Still giving you trouble?" asked Mike. "Oh, you know", replied Arthur, "a little now and then."
"Perhaps you should get a bungalow; walking up and down those stairs can't help".
"Can't see that happening, bungalows are scarce and mostly in up-market neighbourhoods. That puts them out of my price range". They were silent for a few moments. "Well", said Mike eventually, "why not come and live closer to us, we could help out with the chores and do a few odd jobs for you?"
"We've been all over than, son. Living down south was fine while your mum was around, but Preston is where I was born and grew up. I like it here. I do alright; I'm not a bloody invalid..."
"...I wasn't suggesting..." tried Mike. "I'm not a bloody invalid", repeated his father firmly, "I have friends here, and the neighbours are fine. You have enough to do building the business".

"I'd enjoy having you around a bit more", said Mike, genuinely. "Well it's nice of you to say so", replied Arthur, "but things are fine as they are. Now, how's that racer coming on, are you going to win the Targa or not?" Mike started this conversation with his father on a regular basis, and knew that the older man had just closed it - again. Nicola entered carrying a tray containing a steaming hot pot of tea, three cups, a jug of milk, a bowl of sugar and a plate containing a selection of the sweet, sticky cakes beloved of both men. Mike got up, moved a coffee table to within reaching distance of the chairs, and resumed his seat on the sofa. Nicola sat beside him. Mike leaned forward and poured three cups of tea, adding a heaped spoonful of sugar to his own and that of his father, before passing a steaming brew and the plate of cakes to the older man, who took the tea and selected a large sticky bun. Nicola accepted a cup of tea but declined the cakes. "So", said Arthur between mouthfuls of cake, "are you going to win the Targa?"

"Tough call", replied Mike, equally absorbed with a large jam doughnut. "I think the car will be good. We have a test track of sorts laid out on the old airfield runways adjoining the works and I've tried the prototype on that. Of course the runways are dead flat and nothing like the Targa but the car felt good. Very powerful, good handling, so I've arranged a two day private test down at Brands Hatch. That has some humps and bumps, again nothing like the Targa but we should get a better idea there".

"Will you drive in the race?" asked Arthur and before Mike could reply Nicola snapped "No! He won't! He will have too much to do running the team." Mike shot his father a wry look and the older man raised his eyebrows and gave an almost imperceptible shrug of his shoulders. "No", Mike said, "as Nicola says, there will be too much to do, but I'm putting myself down as reserve driver so that I can put in some practice laps and see how the cars are handling".

"Will you go out to Sicily, Nicola?" asked Arthur. "Yes, I hope to", she said, "I've already told them at the office that I want those weeks off, so they've had plenty of warning".

"She'll be invaluable", said Mike, "my schoolboy French never was up to much but Nicola speaks three languages fluently".

"That's right, of course", agreed Arthur, "which ones are they again?" Nicola sipped her tea, enjoying the moment. "French, Spanish, and Italian", she said finally, delicately replacing cup in saucer. There was silence for a few moments as the men devoured the remainder of their cakes, then Mike spoke again. "Dad?" he asked. "Hmm?" replied the older man, finishing his tea. "Do you remember Peter Snelgrove?" At the mention of the name, Arthur Brookes sat back in his chair. "Peter Snelgrove", he said in admiration, "now there was a driver. I saw him race an E.R.A. at Brooklands back in the thirties. The car was an ex Grand Prix model, but outdated, well used, and to make matters worse, owned by a private entrant and run on a shoestring budget. Most racing drivers in those days, your friend Charles Standish included, had wealthy parents or backers, Snelgrove didn't so he had to take whatever was available. He should have been completely outclassed by Mercedes and Auto Union – their cars were superb, their drivers likewise, and the technical back-up they brought with them had to be seen to be believed, fully equipped mobile workshops, armies of mechanics, the lot." Arthur Brookes smiled in recollection, "But oh boy", he continued, "did that race turn out to be a driver's nightmare? Pouring rain one minute, dry the next, and there was Snelgrove, driving like a demon and bringing that E.R.A. home in first place, minutes ahead of the second placed Merc. It was after that drive that Auto Union hired him for their Grand Prix team. I remember the helmet he used when he drove for the Germans, silver, with a Union Jack on one side and a German tricolour on the other. Why d'you ask?"

"His name cropped up".

"Peter Snelgrove", repeated the older man wistfully, "haven't heard of him in years. I heard he spent the war in Switzerland, what's he doing now?"

"No idea", said Mike.

The first day of the Brands Hatch test dawned with typically British early summer weather – dull, overcast, and spotting with rain. A convoy comprising two Bedford lorries, each carrying a precious Pegasus Seafire Mk.II racer, two small vans - one containing spares and equipment, one containing a small cache of racing tyres that Brookes had been able to obtain - a 1951 Vauxhall Wyvern and a pre-war Austin Chummy, both carrying mechanics, turned off the A20 and into the main entrance, drove slowly along the access route that ran behind the spectator stands and parallel to the circuit's main straight, turned left and parked in the paddock area. Mike Brookes and three mechanics got quickly out of the Wyvern and set-to opening the rear doors of the lorries, drawing out wheel ramps from either side of the race cars inside, and placing them level with their rear wheels. Extricating themselves from the tiny Austin Chummy, Alan Francis and Harold Cooper, plus another engineer, stretched cramped muscles and watched the Seafires carefully wheeled down the ramps. Francis licked his lips in an attempt to lubricate a mouth dry with tension and expectation and had to admit that the cars certainly looked superb, sleekly aerodynamic and resplendent in their British racing green livery. Three white decals adorned the bodywork, one on each door, one on the bonnet, awaiting their allotted race numbers.

Despite the fact that this was mid-week Francis had agreed to close the lock-up in Walthamstow so that Charlie Small and Freddie Kendal could be present at the test. Brookes intended to take these two, his best mechanics, to Sicily with the team, and the engineer had no quarrel with that. Now he watched as Freddie, Charlie, and the other mechanics and engineers in oily well-used overalls, fussed around the cars and treated them with as much care and attention as they would lavish on wives and girlfriends. This was scarcely surprising, mused Francis philosophically, since, like all thoroughbreds, the cars would almost certainly prove to be feminine in nature - highly-strung and difficult to please.

Francis watched as Freddie Kendal opened the bonnet of one of the racers to make a few adjustments, while Mike Brookes removed his leather jacket, tossed it into the Wyvern then leaned in to retrieve the claret-coloured racing helmet with the Winged Pegasus logo. Charlie Small arrived at the racer, he and Freddie held a short but animated conversation, and Freddie closed the bonnet. Brookes looked towards them and Charlie gave a thumbs-up. Dressed in shirt and slacks, his only concession to what he was about to undertake being the helmet, which he dropped onto the passenger seat, and a pair of lightweight driving boots, Brookes climbed into the racer and pressed the electric starter. Francis heart thumped in his chest as the big V8 engine, his own creation, stuttered then burst into life and the familiar crisp roar echoed deafeningly around the paddock as Brookes blipped the throttle. Putting the car into reverse, Brookes engaged the clutch and slowly backed and turned the car to face the paddock entrance, then drove slowly out of the paddock and through the underpass than ran under the main straight. Freddie and Charlie having performed their same quick-check routine on the second racer, Charlie jumped into the driver's seat, fired the engine and followed Brookes. Mechanics jumped aboard each van and they moved off after the cars, followed on foot by Alan Francis and assorted engineers.

Mike Brookes drove the car up out of the underpass, behind the pits and pulled into the rear of the first drive-through garage, the front of which faced onto pit lane and access to the race track. Switching off the engine, he heard the low rumble of the second car as Charlie drove it slowly past and into the second garage. Enough room existed for both cars in one garage, but Brookes arranged for the use of two so that mechanics and engineers would have plenty of room in which to work. To the right next to the pits stood race control, looking not unlike the tower of a World War II airfield. Across the track were spectator areas and a stand.

As vans and mechanics arrived and began to set themselves up, Mike Brookes walked along pit lane to take a look around the circuit, which could all be seen from the pits area. The B.R.S.C.C. had plans to more than double the lap length by extending out into the country but for the moment the short but interesting track comprised a main straight which swept up a shallow incline past the start-finish line level with the pits, before dropping away downhill around a sweeping right-hand corner, the demanding Paddock Bend, followed by a short up hill stretch to a right-hand hairpin, Druids. From there it was downhill to a sharpish left hander, a short straight running parallel to and behind the pits, another left hander and a short uphill section to Clearways, a long sweeping right hand bend that led back onto the main pit straight, in all the circuit being more or less kidney shaped. Brookes liked the look of it and waited impatiently as gear was unloaded from vans and last minute checks were carried out on the cars. Finally Alan Francis signalled that all was ready, Brookes glancing up as he walked back at a sky which remained overcast, but the light rain had stopped and the circuit was dry. Brookes stepped into the first garage, retrieved his helmet from the passenger seat of the car, walked around to the driver's side and got in. Stemming from his experiences as a fighter pilot, Brookes had installed a seat harness on the driver's side of the cars, the straps of which came over the shoulders, across the waist and up between the legs of the driver, all held in place by a buckle at the waist. He knew that many race drivers did not like the idea of a harness, believing it to be restrictive, but, whether in an aircraft or a car, he found exerting maximum control to be easier if the inevitable 'G' forces encountered were not causing his butt to slide around in the seat.

With helmet on and harness in place, Brookes pressed the electric starter and the engine burst into life. Easing the car into first gear he edged the powerful machine out of the garage, turned right and accelerated along pit lane. As pit lane merged into the race track Brookes snicked the gear lever up once, twice, and accelerated down around Paddock and up towards Druids Bend.

Brookes took the first couple of laps at medium pace to acclimatise himself to the track and the car, but as he came out of the long right hander onto the main straight for the third time he floored the accelerator and felt the car punch him in the back as it leapt forward. Glancing down at the instrument panel Brookes noticed the rev counter exceed 18,000, but as the car screamed across the start-finish line he felt and heard the engine stutter. Lifting his right foot off the accelerator fractionally, the engine picked up and he accelerated through Paddock, but again the misfire interrupted progress. Brookes slowed and cruised around to the pits with the engine again running unevenly. Stopping outside the garage he lifted the visor on the helmet and undid the chin strap as Alan Francis leaned over. "I know", said the engineer, "misfire, we heard it loud and clear. Hop out and we'll strip down the carbs, there may be a problem with one of them. Try the other car, see how that runs". Brookes tried the second car and encountered the same problem, a nagging misfire at high and low revs. Perplexed, Francis scratched his head. "Well", he said, "we've stripped down and rebuilt the carbs on the first car. Didn't find anything obviously wrong but it may just have been minute particles of grit on one of the needles. Try it again". Brookes tried again and the problem persisted. Back at the pits Brookes leaned against the car and listened intently as Francis, Cooper, and the remaining engineers huddled over the open bonnet and attempted to discover the source of the problem.

Having checked and rechecked the obvious and the not so obvious without result, Francis finally decided on a complete strip-down and rebuild of the fuel and ignition systems, an operation likely to take some time. Faced with this, and unwilling to completely waste the morning, Brookes opted to take out the second car but try as far as possible to keep the revs between 3500 and 18,000, below and above which the misfire seemed to occur.

By now Brookes was becoming used to the circuit and by adapting his driving to the rev limit imposed by the misfire, felt he might still turn in some reasonable laps and gain valuable experience on how the racer behaved when driven in anger. Easing the car out into pit lane, the misfire at low revs now quite noticeable, he glanced into the first garage and saw the car up on ramps with engineers and mechanics swarming around and stripping it down in an attempt to cure the problem. Once onto the track he cruised around until the long right hander before the main straight then accelerated hard up to 18,000, feeling the car surge forward under him. As he topped the rise just beyond the pits he turned right into Paddock and eased off the power to have something in hand with which to accelerate through the corner. Keeping to the 18,000 limit, and starting to enjoy himself immensely, Brookes approached the Druids hairpin, braked with the big toe and left side of his right boot while the right side and heel of the boot hovered over the accelerator. Pushing out the clutch with his left boot he dropped down two gears, and as he allowed the clutch pedal up, his right boot went smoothly back on the power, the car hugging the kerb beautifully. Smiling broadly to himself he changed back up a gear, accelerated down and turned into the left hander at the bottom of the hill. As soon as he turned the wheel the car bit ferociously into the corner and the tail slid out with a screech of tyres. Brookes quickly eased off the power, corrected the slide and with the power back on turned into the second left hander at the end of the short straight. Again the car bit into the corner and the tail slid out. Brookes corrected the slide and drove back to the pits, pulling up outside the second garage. "Problem, guv?" asked Charlie Small, leaning over the car. "Nasty oversteer into left-handers", replied the driver, lifting the visor of the helmet. "Probably a roll bar adjustment", said Charlie and motioned to Freddie to help him, "we'll get 'er up on the ramps and ease it off a notch or two". The two turned to ready the ramps as Brookes pursed his lips. "Charlie", he called. "Guv?" replied the mechanic, turning back. "We may not need all that", continued Brookes, "it could be a balance weight problem. Put more weight into the right front wheel".

"righto" said Charlie as Freddie sprinted to the rear of the garage and returned with a small lead weight weighing no more than a few grams, which he attached to the wheel as directed. "OK", said Freddie standing and giving a thumbs-up, "try that". Brookes snapped down the visor and accelerated away. Now the car handled beautifully and settling to his task he completed the stint by reeling off a long series of laps all within a few fractions of 48 seconds per lap, a good time for the circuit and achieved despite the rev limit. Motoring back to the pits, he stopped and lifted the visor. Charlie and Freddie stood in front of the garage, arms folded. "Better?" asked Charlie, both mechanics grinning broadly. "Better", said Brookes, getting out of the car. "Well", said Charlie, jerking a thumb at the adjoining garage, "that's the good news; you better step next door for the bad news".

Brookes stepped into the next garage and a grease and oil smeared Alan Francis turned to meet him. "Bloody hell, Mike", he said with feeling, "that damn spaceframe might make the car handle like a dream..."
"...it does..."
"...well that's something at least, because it's a bloody nightmare to work around.   Bloody steel tubes everywhere, we had to drop the engine out of the car to be able to do any work on it..."
"But you found the problem?"
"Well I'm pretty sure I have", replied Francis, running a hand through his hair. "And?" asked Brookes. "I think it's because I mounted the carburettors directly onto a solidly based manifold. I'll do some more tests back at the works but I'm fairly certain that engine vibration, particularly at the top and bottom of the rev range, causes petrol in the carbs to froth and results in the misfire. It didn't show up in the dyno tests with the prototype on the test bed, but putting the engine in a car and running it on a track inevitably causes much more movement and vibration - but that's what these shakedowns are for, right?"
"Can you fix it?" asked Brookes anxiously. "Sure", replied Francis, "but not here. I'll have to design a flexible manifold system..."
"How long?"
"With a bit of luck it shouldn't delay the programme by much; I've sketched out a few ideas already. As long as everything checks when I've had a bit of time to work out the details we should have the parts fabricated and on the cars in a week, ten days maybe, no more than that".

"Is running the cars as they are likely to damage the engines?"

"Shouldn't think so, not if you stay within the limits. You'll carry on with the test?"

"Yes", replied Brookes, "we have a couple of drivers coming down tomorrow, we'll explain the rev limits to them and let them have a run. It'll be good discipline for them, we'll see if they have a brain in their heads, because it's going to take more than just a lead right boot to tackle the Targa".

Following the consumption of prodigious quantities of sandwiches and Coke for lunch, the team got back to work. Alan Francis and the engineers began the laborious job of rebuilding their car while Brookes settled down to put in many more laps in his. Drawing on previous racing experience, the Pegasus boss tried different suspension setups and tyre types on the car and began to get a real feel for how it behaved. On towards the end of the session the clouds cleared, the sun appeared for a glorious summer evening, and Brookes put in ten laps in the neighbourhood of 47 seconds. Emerging from the car he flipped up the visor and undid the chin strap on the helmet as Alan Francis looked up from supervising the finishing touches to his rebuild. "If you can fix that bloody misfire", said Brookes, grinning broadly while stooping to pat the car's bonnet affectionately, "we're going to beat crap out of the competition with this beauty!" Mechanics and engineers alike all caught the mood and a background hum of excited chatter accompanied the business of clearing up for the day.

With the racers safely locked away in the lorries and one van parked alongside them in the paddock, Brookes, Francis, Cooper and an engineer shoehorned themselves into the Austin Chummy, while Freddie Kendal ensconced himself in the driving seat of the Wyvern and the rest of the crew sorted themselves out between that and the remaining van, driven by Charlie Small. Not being able to find a single overnight stopover large enough to accommodate the whole crew locally, Brookes had Jeanine, the Pegasus secretary, book two hostelries a few miles apart along the A20. Alan Francis drove to the Brands Hatch main entrance and turned left, while behind the Austin Freddie Kendal flashed the lights of the Wyvern and turned right, followed by the van.

With dusk beginning to fall the Austin Chummy turned into the car park of a large country pub along the A20 and drew to a halt. The four occupants extricated themselves from the cramped interior, retrieved overnight bags from the boot and marched purposefully into the pub, looking forward to a cool pint or two and a good meal.

Washed and changed the four met in the bar, Francis and Cooper perched on bar stools while Brookes got the beers in and Alan Francis pulled an already much folded piece of paper from his pocket and laid it on the bar counter. The paper contained his outline sketch and specification for the flexible manifold, and the three engineers immediately went into a huddle to discuss the pros and cons of this or that, while Brookes asked questions from the sidelines. With Cooper getting the second round in and Francis the third, the solution to the misfire seemed, at least in theory, to be at hand, and the four potential World Sports Car Champions were feeling no pain at all.

"Any chance an outsider might get into to this testosterone club?" asked a familiar voice, and Brookes turned. "Nicola!" he said, "you made it!" and he put his arm around her and gave her a hug. Alan Francis stood next to Brookes and offered Nicola the seat, which she took. "You mean to tell me", he said to his companion in a stage whisper, while winking at the engineers, "you let Nicola drive that Seafire of yours all the way down here?"

"Of course", replied Brookes, "why not?"

"Well", continued Francis, "it must be love, that's all I can say".

"Pack it in you two", said Nicola, "I girl could die of thirst waiting for a drink here". Quickly fortified by a gin and tonic the new arrival asked how the day had gone. "Stirling Moss here", Francis said, indicating Brookes, "had the time of his life swanning around Brands while we all barked the skin off our knuckles trying to get past his chassis to work on the engine". Brookes shot his companion a wry look and gave him a dig in the ribs. "Had my colleague here's engine worked…" he began. "OK boys", said Nicola, "I can see it can't have been too bad. Can we get anything to eat here?"

"Sure", said Brookes, "and I think we're all about ready". The men nodded hungrily and finished their drinks, Nicola picked up her gin and tonic and they trooped through to the restaurant.

The pub menu was simple but the food was good, well cooked, and there was plenty of it. After the meal the three engineers returned to the bar, while Brookes took Nicola by the arm and they stepped out into the cool summer evening. With all trace of clouds by now a memory, a thousand stars twinkled in the deepening blue of the oncoming night. Brookes put his arm around the girl's waist and the two walked slowly around to a small garden area laid out with tables and chairs, and occupied by a few patrons. Not speaking, her head lying on his shoulder, they continued their walk, the scent of newly mown grass and rose blossom filling the air. Eventually they returned to the pub entrance and turned to face each other. Nicola snuggled against him and he felt her firm body through her thin summer dress. "Why Mister Brookes", she said softly and teasingly, "does driving racing cars always make you this horny?"

"Always", he said, and they turned and walked back into the pub and up to their room.

7

The second day of the test dawned bright, clear, and warm. Following a traditional English breakfast of eggs, bacon, tomatoes, and numerous of cups of tea, Mike Brookes and the crew headed back to Brands Hatch. Accompanied by Nicola in the Seafire and followed by Alan Francis and the engineers in the Chummy, Brookes drove into the circuit entrance and along to the paddock, discovering the Wyvern already there and Freddie Kendal and the mechanics already at work unloading race cars from lorries. Brookes and Francis parked alongside. "Everything OK, Freddie?" asked Brookes, getting out of the car. "No problems", replied the mechanic. The Pegasus director looked the crew over, "one or two of the boys look a bit second hand", he said critically. "Oh, they'll be OK", offered Freddie, "they had a pint or two, but nobody got really legless".

"Where's Charlie?" asked Brookes, glancing about, "I don't see him".

"Oh he hooked up with one of the barmaids", smiled Freddie, "but he'll be along shortly. I've seen him this morning; he has to put some petrol in the van". Brookes smiled wryly. "Barmaid eh?" he mused, "I don't know where he gets the stamina", then taking a deep breath of country fresh morning air he clapped his hands and rubbed them together. "Right", he said, "let's get the cars over to the pits and get started".

With the racers in pit lane and mechanics and engineers checking them over, Charlie Small arrived in the van to an accompaniment of catcalls and much ribald comment – although cleaned up for the benefit of Nicola, who stood in the entrance to the first garage enjoying the moment along with everyone else. Getting out of the van Small walked along pit lane smiling sheepishly and followed by much banter and back-slapping. "'Morning guv", he said, arriving in front of Brooks.

" 'Morning Casanova".

"Ah, you heard", continued Charlie with hands in the pockets of his overalls and shuffling nervously from foot to foot, "sorry I'm late, had to get some petrol for the van".

"I heard that as well", said Brooks. "Well, now you're here I'd like you to get to work on the car I used yesterday, see it's all ready to go and we'll use that for the driver tests today, it will make a useful comparison". Charlie turned to the car and then turned back, "Guv?" he asked. "Yes Charlie", replied Brooks. "Who are the two blokes wandering about behind the stands?" asked the mechanic.

"Two blokes", asked Brookes, "what two blokes?"

"Well", continued Charlie, "one's a tall guy, a bit older than you, you know, middle aged..."

"...careful Charlie, you're already on thin ice..."

"...sorry guv, anyway the tall one's got a helmet bag, the other one's older".

"Well", said Brooks, "if one of them has a helmet bag he must be one of the drivers coming for a test".

"Want me to go and get them?"

"I think we'll see if they can find their way over here, shall we? After all if they can't do that there's no point me letting them loose in the mountains of Sicily is there?" The mechanic gave a chuckle, "no guv", he replied, "I'll get to work".

Brookes took out the racer that had been rebuilt the previous day and did a number of exploratory laps to see how it compared to the sister car, then brought it in and parked it in the first garage. As he stood discussing a number of handling and engine performance issues with Alan Francis, Freddie Kendal tapped him on the shoulder, "visitors", said the mechanic and pointed across the track. Brookes glanced to where Kendal pointed and saw two young men in slacks and shirts. Both carried racing helmets. "That must be our test drivers", mused the Pegasus director and he stepped past Kendal and Francis to walk across the track and meet the new arrivals. "'Morning", he said, "Mike Brookes of Pegasus, can I help you?" The first man, in his early twenties, a little shorter than Brookes, with dark, slicked down hair, stuck out his hand, "Mister Brookes, pleased to meet you, I'm Adrian Rawnsley-Bysh"; he said in perfect Oxbridge, "I believe we have a mutual friend in Sir Charles Standish". Brookes shook the proffered hand. "And this", continued Rawnsley-Bysh, "is Piers Furnley of..."

"...the Furnley Shipping Company?" asked Brookes. "Absolutely", confirmed the second arrival, also shaking Brookes' hand. Of similar build to Rawnsley-Bysh, but with curly brown hair, Furnley displayed a virtually identical cut-glass accent. "Well gentlemen", said Brookes, "I see you've brought your helmets so you know what you're here for, but before we start you'd better give me some idea of what racing experience you have."

"Yes", started Rawnsley-Bysh, "well, we've done a lot of 500c.c. racing..."

"...these are a bit more potent than 500c.c. racers", interrupted Brookes, jerking a thumb over his shoulder at the pits. "Oh absolutely", continued Rawnsley-Bysh, "we also campaigned a two-litre Triumph TR2 in a few of the 'fifty-four World Sports Car Championship races, including the Le Mans twenty-four hours".

"How did you do?"

"At Le Mans?" Asked Furnley, then answered his own question, "we went out after ten hours or so, oil pressure".

"Bad luck. Where were you placed when you went out?"

"Eighteenth", replied Rawnsley-Bysh, "but I think we could have done better had the car kept going".

"All racing drivers think that", said Brookes with a smile, "still, eighteenth in a TR2 after ten hours wasn't too bad".

"And the Targa doesn't last as long as Le Mans does it?" asked Furnley. "Who told you we were entering the Targa Florio?" responded Brookes quickly. "Oh, I think Sir Charles might have mentioned it", replied Rawnsley-Bysh. "Well I would rather he hadn't", snapped the Pegasus boss, "I don't want anything about this project getting out until we've done a lot more development and we are a lot closer to the race date". Brookes ran a hand through his hair, annoyed that the Lynx Chairman had not heeded his warnings concerning confidentiality. "And to answer your question", he said, indicating Furnley, "no, it doesn't last as long as Le Mans, and it isn't on a billiard-ball smooth race track either, it's eight hours or more of competing against the best cars and drivers in the world over the most difficult and dangerous roads you'll ever have to race on. *If* you get the drive, this will be the toughest event you'll ever be in". An awkward silence showed signs of mushrooming until Furnley coughed nervously. "Uh I believe", he said, attempting to re-start the conversation, "that I read somewhere that you drove at Le Mans as well, a few years before us, and had a bit of an experience along Mulsanne". Brookes was prepared to allow himself to be mollified this time and his face broke into a wry smile. "Yes", he replied, "it had been raining and just before midnight as I turned into the Mulsanne straight a fuse blew, water must have seeped into the electrics somehow. The engine kept going but all the lights, headlights, dashboard lights, the lot, failed".

"What did you do?" asked Furnley. "I drove by the lights of the car in front", mused Brookes, "kept on his tail and tried to pinpoint where I was. I saw his brake lights come on for the sharp right-hander at the end of the straight and after that it wasn't so bad as there were a few trackside lights to drive back to the pits by".

"Tough break" continued Furnley. "Character building", replied the Pegasus director laconically, "but I understand driving without lights at night is actually a tactic used by some drivers in the Mille Miglia and other overnight road races so that the guy in front can't keep track of how close you are". Brookes turned back toward the pits and was silent for a moment. "OK", he said over his shoulder at last, "let's see what you can do", and he led the way back across the track.

Arriving at the pits Brookes confirmed that the car selected for the test was ready and Rawnsley-Bysh climbed into the driving seat, strapped on his helmet and flipped down the visor. Brookes explained the rev limit in force and that a waved chequered flag from the pits meant that he should bring the car in. Buckling up the seat harness at Brookes insistence, Rawnsley-Bysh took the car out onto the track and dropping down through Paddock, accelerated hard up the short straight to Druid's hairpin to a screech of tyres and a plume of grey tyre smoke as the driver stepped hard on the brakes. Progress around the hairpin was accompanied by more screeching of tyres and as the car came out onto the short downhill straight the tail slid out. The driver corrected the slide then completed the lap with more of the same and blasted across the start-finish line to start his second lap. Brookes turned from the pit wall to Nicola, who held the clipboard to which was attached two stop watches and the lap chart. He raised his eyebrows. "Fifty-two seconds" she said. Rawnsley-Bysh completed the second lap in much the same style as the first, for a time of pretty much the same. "No, no", Brookes said to Alan Francis, "he's trying too hard; he needs to relax a bit". Turning to Charlie Small Brookes told him to scoot down to the back straight behind the pits and wave the flag to bring the car in. Rawnsley-Bysh duly cruised back into pit lane and flipped up the visor to his helmet as Brookes squatted on his haunches beside the car. "Try to make your laps a bit smoother", he said, "you're losing time with all that sliding about and tyre smoking stuff".

"What time did I do?"

"Fifty-two".

"Have you driven the car here?"

"Yes", confirmed Brookes, "yesterday".

"What times did you do?"

"I put in some laps at forty-seven". Rawnsley-Bysh wiped a hand across his forehead. "It's very twitchy under braking", he said, "and there's quite a vibration up through the steering".

"I'm not surprised", replied Brookes, "the way you slammed on the anchors up at Druids I expect you've flat-spotted a tyre. Now, have another go and take it a bit easier this time, get used to the car before you start trying to break the lap record, and if the vibration's too bad, come back in and we'll check the tyres".

Brookes watched as the car edged out onto the track again, then stood by Nicola as she filled in the chart, lap by lap. Rawnsley-Bysh took it easier this time, allowing time to bed himself in. He had just completed a lap at 49.5 seconds when Brookes became aware of a commotion further along pit lane. Glancing up from the lap chart he noticed Charlie Small, Freddie Kendal, and several other mechanics grouped together and talking in hushed but excited tones about something on the other side of the track. Brookes followed their line of sight and even at this distance she was gorgeous. Dressed in elegantly casual slacks and blouse she was tall, with long black hair and a figure that Venus de Milo would happily give her arms for. She stood in the front row of one of the spectator stands, and she was with Mark Spall. "I say", said Piers Furnley, who had been standing nearby, "that's Gina d'Alessandro isn't it?"

"You know her?" asked Brookes. "Lord yes", continued Furnley appreciatively, "she's Italian, a freelance journalist, she interviewed us at Le Mans. She gets a lot of stuff printed in Italian magazines, motoring and lifestyle, you know the sort of thing. She's very good, gets a lot more from the motoring boys than male journalists, as you can probably imagine".

"I'll bloody murder him", muttered Brookes and strode to the pit wall. Making sure the car was nowhere near the main straight he leapt over the wall and sprinted across the track. "Did I say something wrong?" asked Furnley and Nicola smiled. "We could be in for a firework or two", she said.

Brookes strode across the track and stepped through a gap in the wall on the far side. Smiling benignly, Spall came to the end of the row of seats to meet him. "Mike..." he said, and Brookes grabbed his arm, spun him around and pushed him back up the steps between the rows of seating. Finally he stopped and stood in front of the finance director. "What the bloody hell do you think you're doing?" he asked with barely suppressed fury. "Mike, that's..." began Spall. "I *know* who the bloody hell it is! What's she doing *here!* This is supposed to be a private test session, and you've brought along a bloody journalist, an *Italian* journalist no less! We'll be in next month's motoring magazines all over bloody Europe!"

"Hey, Mike", said Spall, withered by Brookes evident displeasure, "I don't think..."

"Exactly!" spat Brookes angrily. Spall opened his mouth to speak again, but the incandescent Pegasus director cut him off. "Keep her away from the test", he breathed. "I don't want to see her on the other side of that race track or anywhere near any of the crew! Got it!" Spall nodded and Brookes strode back down the steps. As he drew level with d'Alessandro she moved to the end of the row and thrust out her hand. "Mister Brookes?" she asked, the voice soft and modulated by a delectable Italian accent, "It is Mister Brookes is it not? It is so nice to meet you". Brookes took the hand and gave it a perfunctory shake, at the same time noticing her smooth olive tanned complexion and deep, very deep, brown eyes. He felt a stirring in his loins, was annoyed at the reflex response and even more annoyed that it was obvious from her Mona Lisa smile that she was perfectly well aware of the reaction she was getting. He turned to the track, watched the car pull slowly into pit lane and stomped angrily back across to the pits. By the time he arrived Rawnsley-Bysh had the visor of his helmet up and was talking with Alan Francis.

79

"Well, what is it?" asked Brookes shortly. Francis turned, "vibration", he said, "I expect..."

"He's flat-spotted a bloody tyre", snapped Brookes, "...he's flat spotted a tyre" finished Francis wryly. Brookes turned on his heel, "hey!" he called to the mechanics, "if you've finished standing around drooling we need the front tyres here checked and changed!" It was obvious from the tone that this statement was not up for discussion so Small, Kendal, and the others swarmed around the car and as Rawnsley-Bysh stepped out, had it up on jacks and the front wheels off. Brookes turned again and walked through to the back of the garage to take a few deep breaths and recover from how angry he was with Mark Spall. Feeling his pulse rate drop, he walked slowly back to where Nicola held the lap chart, while both drivers and Alan Francis studied it. "How did it go?" asked Brookes. "He did a forty-eight-and-a-half", offered Nicola, and Brookes held out his hand. Nicola passed him the chart and he ran his eye quickly down the times. "What about the tyres?" he asked and Freddie Kendal looked up from where he and Charlie were checking them over. "Driver's side front is flat-spotted", he said, "it probably caused quite a judder through the steering".

"I expect that affected my times", said Rawnsley-Bysh. "Yes", said Brookes, "I expect it did, but you shouldn't have braked so hard that you locked the wheels up in the first place". Brookes was calmer now, but knew that if he was to get anything from these drivers he could not afford to pussy-foot around with them. "Also", he continued, "your times are all over the place. You did fifteen laps; your best time was on the tenth lap, with those around it anything up to half a second adrift". Brookes handed the chart to Rawnsley-Bysh. "With more practice in the car you'll get quicker, of that I have no doubt. What I'm not at all certain about, however, is whether you can put in quick laps consistently, for hour after hour". The young man was evidently not used to being spoken to this way and flushed. "Let me try again", he said, and his voice cracked with the emotion of bruised pride. "Maybe later", said Brookes, "Furnley, when the car's ready, take it out and see what you can do". Furnley nodded and pulled on his helmet while Brookes took Nicola by the arm and led her a short distance away. "Look", he said quietly, "that idiot Mark has brought along an Italian journalist..."

"Good looking one too", she quipped. "Oh don't you start", he said irritably, "go and have a word with her, practice your Italian, see if you can find out what she's up to, and keep her as far as possible away from the test, OK?"

"OK", she said, "by the way, what's her name? Mata Hari?"

"Very funny. It's Gina, Gina d'Alessandro". Nicola handed Brookes the lap chart and behind them the car fired up and Furnley drove along pit lane and out onto the track.

Furnley put in an extended stint and got down to forty-nine seconds but, unlike his compatriot, once settled in he proved to be consistent, managing a string of laps within a fraction of a second of his quickest time. At one point the engine stuttered as the driver topped the 18,000 rev limit but Furnley quickly backed off and did not repeat the error. Not too displeased with the performance, Brookes had Charlie Small hang out the chequered flag and brought the morning session to a close. Glancing across the track, he noticed Nicola following Mark Spall and Gina out of the stand. Quickly she turned and indicated that she was taking them for lunch, presumably at the pub at which she and Brookes had stayed the previous night.

In the pits packed lunches were produced courtesy of the hostelries at which they had stayed the previous night. Mechanics and engineers got into huddles at which the talk was as much of the shapely Ms d'Alessandro as it was of cars, while Alan Francis pored over notes he had been making concerning engine performance, and over by the race car they had used, Andrew Rawnsley-Bysh and Piers Furnley talked over their morning's work. Standing with his back to the pit wall taking all this in while munching a sandwich, Mike Brookes mentally flipped through the long list of things he had to do by yesterday at the very latest in order to make the team competitive. Lost in thought, the Pegasus director barely noticed Charlie Small stand beside him and lean on the pit wall until the mechanic tapped him on the arm. "They're back", he said. ""Hm? grunted Brookes, "who's back?"

"Those two blokes I told you about this morning". So saying Small waved a sandwich in the direction of the stands across the track. Brookes turned and sure enough two men sat watching from several rows back. "I don't believe this", muttered Brookes, "we're supposed to be having a private test session. For all the spectators turning up we might as well have held it during practice for the bloody Grand Prix!" The mechanic smiled, "wonder who they are", he said, "especially the one with the helmet bag. We expecting any more drivers guv?"

"Not that I invited", said Brookes, "but they wouldn't be the first to turn up today uninvited. Still, suppose I'd better go and find out what the hell they want". Mike Brookes finished the sandwich, sat on the pit wall, swung his legs over and walked across the track toward the stands. As he got closer and walked through the gap in the wall on the other side, he eyed the two new arrivals and something tripped a switch in his memory.

Entering the row of seats he sat down beside them, the one closest being tall, a few years older than himself, with a sallow complexion, thinning brown hair and the helmet bag on his lap. The other was in his fifties, with a thin moustache, and wearing glasses. A cigarette in his right hand and nicotine on the fingers told their chain-smoker story. " 'Afternoon", said Brookes, and both the new arrivals nodded. "May I?" asked Brookes, pointing at the helmet bag. "Go ahead", replied the man, the voice subdued and perhaps a little tired sounding, but firm despite his somewhat sickly appearance. Brookes took the bag, opened it and removed the silver open face helmet with the Union Jack on one side and the German tricolour on the other. "Peter Snelgrove", he said. The man glanced toward him, nodded, and they shook hands. "This is George Stepanek", said Snelgrove, indicating the older man, "he was my race mechanic at Auto Union and later for most of my time with Mercedes". Brookes reached across; the man placed the cigarette between his lips and shook hands with the Pegasus director. Brookes tapped the tricolour on the helmet, "how did this go down with your ex bosses?" he asked, and the flicker of a smile played around Snelgrove's lips. "They would have preferred a swastika", he replied with a shrug, "but I kept winning races for them so they let it go. Everybody loves a winner, the Nazis were no different".
"You've been here all day", said Brookes, "why didn't you come over?"
"I wasn't invited", replied Snelgrove matter-of-factly.
"No", agreed Brookes, "still, having come all the way down

here you might have made yourself known". Snelgrove inhaled deeply. "Maybe I'm losing my self-confidence", he murmured, and taking back his helmet he replaced it in the bag and zipped it up. "Time was I'd have bustled over there full of chat and charm and blagged my way into a drive. I suppose I've had too many knock-backs since the war. Nobody wants to know a driver who won races for the Nazi propaganda machine". Again the wan smile played around Snelgrove's lips. "A year or two ago", he said, "I did the same thing as this, turned up unannounced for a team test day at Silverstone and tried to get a drive. The team manager took me aside and explained quietly and patiently how it would be politically unacceptable to give me a drive, 'it's too soon after the war old boy', he said. Then he got into his Mercedes and drove off". Brookes smiled. "Where were you all morning?" he asked, and Snelgrove nodded his head away to his left. "Down at Paddock, watching", he said, and a flicker of interest rekindled in his voice. "And?" the Pegasus director asked. "The car looks promising", Snelgrove replied, the enthusiasm in his voice building, almost despite himself, "but George thinks you haven't got it set up right for Brands - you know, differential ratios, that sort of thing". Brookes glanced across at the older man. "George is quite right", he said, "but we're not going to be racing here. This test is just to make sure the wheels go round, we'll do the detailed stuff later. What about the drivers?" At this Snelgrove pursed his lips. "If you do a lot of work with them, give them lots of practice in the cars they might get you a place in the top ten or fifteen".

"Top ten or fifteen in what?"

"The word is you're going to enter the Targa Florio". Brookes laughed out loud and stood up. "That must be the worst kept secret in motor racing" he chuckled, "especially after this morning", and so saying he stepped to the end of the row of seats. Turning back he spoke again, "come over and have a bite of lunch before the boys scoff it all" he offered. "Kind of you", replied Snelgrove, looking straight ahead, "but we'd better be getting back to London".

"That's a pity" Brookes smiled, "because if you're driving back to London you can't be test driving my race car here, can you?" Snelgrove looked up sharply. "You mean it?" he asked. "You have quite a reputation as a driver", the Pegasus director continued, "and that obviously interests me, but reputations count for nothing on the track so this afternoon you'll have to prove it all over again - If you think you can". Snelgrove looked down at the bag and gently tapped it with the fingers of one hand, his lips pursed as if deep in thought. "I haven't driven a race car for a long time" he murmured, as much to himself as to anyone else. Finally he appeared to come to a decision, picked up the bag and stood. Stepanek dropped the cigarette, stamped it out, and both men followed Brookes as he walked back down the steps. Out on the track Brookes waited until they caught up, "did you ever compete in the Targa?" he asked Snelgrove. "No", the driver replied, "I was due to enter the 1940 event for Mercedes but a World War got in the way". Brookes chuckled. "Pity though", he mused, "we could have used an experienced head in the team".

"Perhaps you should talk to George", Snelgrove said, "he was a race mechanic with Alfa Romeo for the 1935 event and Maserati for the 1939 event". Brookes glanced across, "is that right, George?"

"It is true", said Stepanek, his voice thick with an accent that Brookes could not quite place. "I was with Alfa when they were first and second with Brivio and Chiron in 1935, but the 1939 race barely deserves the name. It did not take place on the magnificent Piccolo Madonie circuit, but on a, oh, what is the phrase you British drivers use?" Snelgrove smiled, "Mickey Mouse", he said. "Yes, yes", continued Stepanek, "that is exactly right, it was on a Mickey Mouse circuit around a park in Palermo. It was all very disappointing, but in any event I had other reasons for being there".

"Oh?" queried Brookes as they reached the pit wall and crossed over. "It's a long story", said Snelgrove and Brookes turned to approach the crew. Clapping his hands to get their attention, he spoke. "OK lads", he said, "if you haven't wolfed the lot can we rustle up a sandwich or two for our guests, Peter Snelgrove and George Stepanek".

"Peter Snelgrove", repeated Charlie Small with something akin to wonder in his voice, "the racing driver?" Snelgrove nodded and made no comment, but some way behind him Rawnsley-Bysh snorted derisively, "he's no racing driver", he said, "he's a bloody has-been!" Snelgrove affected not to have heard and Brookes chose to say nothing for the time being, both knowing full well where the only answer lay and both unsure as to how effective an answer it might now be.

The visitors ate sandwiches and drank Coke and chatted amiably with the crew, although Rawnsley-Bysh remained conspicuously aloof. Furnley remained with his friend although the occasional wistful glance in the direction of the animated group around the new arrivals belied a desire to talk racing with a genuine superstar of the days before the war.

With lunch over Nicola returned to the pits, leaving Gina and Mark Spall in the stands on the opposite side of the track. Brookes was not at all keen that the journalist should see the afternoon session, but was also loath to have Spall take her away. Hell hath no fury etcetera and he had no desire to risk bad publicity with sponsors still to find.

Finally it was time for all, not least Peter Snelgrove himself, to see if he still had anything to offer following his long, enforced, retirement. Sliding his tall frame into the car for the first time he found the leg room cramped, and emerged again so that the seat could be adjusted. For the second time he settled himself into the car and this time professed himself happy. A mechanic stepped forward and coupled up the harness while Brookes squatted by the car to explain the rev limit and he and Snelgrove went quickly over the dashboard layout, oil pressure, engine temperature, and other preparatory checks. With the preliminaries complete, Snelgrove put on the helmet, buckled up the chin strap, put on the goggles and pressed the electric starter on the dash. The engine burst into life and the driver blipped the throttle prior to moving off, the crisp blast of the big three-litre motor echoing around the quiet Kent countryside. By now there was an air of excited expectation in the pit lane that was almost tangible. Mechanics and engineers talked animatedly of the likely outcome of the test, and Snelgrove selected first gear and cruised out of pit lane onto the track.

Armed with the clipboard and stopwatches, Nicola took pride of place along the pit wall opposite the start-finish line, with Brookes, Rawnsley-Bysh, Furnley, and Alan Francis in close attendance. Elsewhere along the wall mechanics and engineers jostled for a good view of the main straight and waited, conversation hushed. The car swept down through Paddock, up around the hairpin, down the back straight, around the long right-hander at Clearways and back down the main straight. Along the wall everyone waited with baited breath. "Fifty-two seconds", said Nicola, and they went back to watching and waiting. The second lap was marginally faster at fifty-one-and-a-half. Three further laps followed at similar times and the excitement along the wall began to abate. "Told you", said Rawnsley-Bysh, "bloody has-been", and he turned away with studied disinterest. The sixth lap came in at fifty seconds dead and mechanics began to drift away from the wall and back to their tasks. Brookes remained alongside Nicola, and further along the pit wall George Stepanek still watched, his fists clenched as if willing an unlikely miracle. Coming around the long right hander before the main straight for the seventh time, the engine note rose and the car streaked across the start-finish line. Nicola was about to read off the time but Brookes cut her short, "never mind", he said, "the next one is the one to watch". Snelgrove lifted slightly for the entrance to Paddock, and accelerated through the corner and up to Druids. Tyres screeched as he found their limit of adhesion and held the car balanced on that razor-edge around the hairpin. Accelerating down and around the left-hander the car came down onto the straight behind the pits and Brookes stepped back to look through the garage as Snelgrove took the car around the second left-hander and out onto the long right-hand bend before the straight. Mechanics and engineers noticed Brookes increased attention and wandered back to the pit wall, while the Pegasus director returned to Nicola's side as the car blasted across the star-finish line once again. "Forty-eight seconds", she said, the surprise evident in her voice. Now car and driver seemed almost to have become one entity. The next lap came in at forty-seven-and-a-half, the next two as close to forty-seven as made no difference. Watching Snelgrove's performance avidly, Brookes found himself torn between his two identities. As a racing driver he had no desire to see his time beaten, but as a designer he desperately wanted to see what a truly world-class driver could do with his car. An excited tension in the pit of his stomach told him that he might just be about to find out.

With the pit wall once again crowded, Snelgrove put in a lap at forty-six-and-a-half, a string of laps at forty-six, and as a final flourish, two laps within fractions of a second of forty-five-and-a-half, all the time appearing to be unhurried and driving well within himself. That told Brookes two things, firstly that Snelgrove still had it in him to be a world class driver, secondly, and for Pegasus perhaps more importantly, that they had a world class car on their hands.

Snelgrove pulled the car slowly into pit lane and came to a halt outside the garage. Switching off the engine he pulled up his goggles and undid the chinstrap. Freddie Kendal stepped forward to undo the harness and the tall driver stepped out of the car and removed the silver helmet. "How was it?" asked Brookes, and the driver smiled. "Handles beautifully", he said, "needs decent tyres of course and a few tweaks here and there but still, it's quite a car..."

"That's all very well," cut in Rawnsley-Bysh sharply, "but what about when you really get on the brakes". Snelgrove glanced in the younger man's direction. "I didn't have to really get on the brakes", he replied conversationally, "but then I'm not a racing driver, I'm a has-been". Rawnsley-Bysh flushed red and turned away, accompanied by one or two sniggers from the crew. Brookes took Snelgrove by the arm, led him over to the pit wall and was followed by Stepanek. "How were my times?" asked the driver. "Quickest were a couple at forty-five-and-a-half".

"The last two", responded Snelgrove. "That's right", continued Brookes, "but most importantly, apart from the few laps you did acclimatising yourself, you were consistently quick".

"Well?" asked Snelgrove, "what do you think?"

"I think you're a bloody fine driver", said Brookes, "and as for giving you a drive, I'd love to".

"But..." said Snelgrove, and Brookes looked him in the eyes. "Yes", he said "frankly there is a problem. We're in the process of bringing commercial sponsors in to help with the financing. Without them I doubt we'll be able to afford to go to Sicily at all. Now, rightly or wrongly..."

"I have a reputation", cut in Snelgrove, the voice suddenly tired again. "I'm the British driver who won races for the Nazis". Turning, he swung over the pit wall and walked slowly across the track. Brookes swore softly. "Mister Brookes", Stepanek said, and the Pegasus director started, unaware that the engineer had been standing close by. "George", he began, "look..."

"Mister Brookes", Stepanek repeated, "you find out what happened in those days, you find out why he spent the war in Switzerland. You need him Mister Brookes; the car is fine, sure, but you need a driver who can get the best from it. He can win this Sicilian race for you and I think now you have seen him you know that, so you find out".

"Is he on the telephone?" asked Brookes. "No", replied the engineer, "but I am, I give you my number and you contact me. Peter deserves this chance; it may be his last, so you 'phone me please". Stepanek scribbled the number on a piece of paper and handed it over, then in turn swung over the pit wall and hurried after Snelgrove. Deep in thought, Brookes turned to walk back to the car only to find Rawnsley-Bysh blocking his way. "Mister Brookes", said the driver, "you must give me another chance to show what I can do".

"I don't think so", replied the Pegasus boss, pushing past, "I think I've seen enough". Again Rawnsley-Bysh blocked his way. "Mister Brookes, please" he pleaded, "one more chance". Nearby, and stooping over the engine bay of the car, Alan Francis straightened up. "If they've got anything at all to offer as drivers, Snelgrove should have given them both plenty to think about", he said, "so why not give them another run? The car's ready to go and we might as well make the best use of the track while we've got it to ourselves." Brookes scratched his head. "OK", he said finally, and pointed to Rawnsley-Bysh, "you first". Eagerly the young driver dashed off to the garage and returned, putting on his helmet and tightening up the chinstrap. Getting into the car, Rawnsley-Bysh flipped down the visor, Freddie Kendal buckled up the harness and Brookes squatted beside the car. "Remember", he said, "nothing has changed from this morning, get yourself settled in before you start charging around, and remember there's still a rev limit". The driver nodded, pressed the starter, selected first gear and the car growled along pit lane and out onto the track.

Brookes and Francis stood with Nicola by the pit wall, while Small and Kendal wandered out through the garage to watch the car down through Paddock and up around Druids. Rawnsley-Bysh appeared to be making some attempt to tidy up his driving, but whereas Snelgrove held the car on the limit of adhesion, the younger man still spent too much time sliding it around for Brookes' liking. Still, as Nicola read off the lap times, they showed some improvement, two within fractions of a second of forty-nine and the third at forty-eight-and-a-half. Laps at forty-eight and forty-seven-and-a-half followed, but the engine stuttered into Paddock as the driver exceeded the rev limit in his efforts to find more speed. On the next lap the car blasted across the start-finish line for another forty-seven-and-a-half, but as it disappeared from view behind the control tower, down into Paddock the engine again stuttered but this time Rawnsley-Bysh did not lift off and tried instead to accelerate through. The engine cut completely and in pit lane they heard a screech of tyres followed by a heavy 'crump', and watched as a cloud of dust arose from the direction of the corner. Charlie Small cantered back through the garage. "He dropped it going through Paddock", said the mechanic dryly, "stuffed it into the scenery on the outside of the corner".
"Is he OK?" called Brookes, and still standing at the back of the garage, Freddie Kendal gave the thumbs-up. "He's out and walking around", he called back. "Charlie", Brookes said to the mechanic, "take Freddie, a van and a

tow-rope and go get the stupid bastard." As his glance shifted to Alan Francis, the engineer shrugged. "Any more bright ideas?" Brookes asked.

Turning to Nicola, he leaned on the pit wall and gazed across the track as Gina d'Alessandro and Mark Spall walked slowly out of the stand. "So?" he asked, "what's Mata Hari's story?" and Nicola smiled. "She says she's working freelance on a piece covering the rise of the new generation of British racers. You know, Lotus, Cooper, and now us".
"And Mark?"
"Well he's certainly screwing her, if that's what you mean".
"Oh perfect", groaned Brookes, "just bloody perfect!"

8

By the time George Stepanek was halfway across the track he had a fresh cigarette alight and parked between his lips. In the stands watching first Snelgrove and then the engineer walk by, Gina turned to Mark Spall. "Mark, who is the tall one?" she asked, "the driver, he is familiar, I think I should know him".

"No idea", replied Spall truthfully, "as far as I knew we only had the other two down to test here today".

"He is very good", she said, "very quick. Can you find out more, for my article?"

"Well I'll try", smiled Mark, "but not just now. I don't think Mike is too chuffed about me bringing a journalist here at all". She pouted deliciously, "oh Mark", she breathed, "I am just a journalist to you?"

"Cut it out", he said, "stop taking the Mickey". Hands on hips, she raised her eyebrows. "Taking the Mickey?" she repeated questioningly, "what is this taking the Mickey?"

"Trying to make me look a bloody idiot", he replied, smiling. "Markie", she said, her voice low and sultry, her arm slipping around his, "you don't need my help for that". Taking mock offence he put his nose in the air and turned away. Giggling, she led the way out of the row of seats and on to the steps, the roar of the car once again out on the track accompanying their departure. "Now", she said, "let us see if we can catch up with our mystery driver", but Mark hung back. "Look", he replied, "I don't want to tread on Mike Brookes' toes, if he wants that kept a secret, that's fine with me".

"Oh but Mark", she cajoled, "what about my article, you promised you would help me". Behind them they heard the engine cut, the tyres screech and the heavy 'thump' as

Rawnsley-Bysh made the lightening transformation from driver to passenger and rode the car into the earth bank. Spall winced. "And I will", he said, "but not today, definitely not today".

It was a hot summer's day and the Lynx boardroom was stuffy. Mike Brookes opened a window and looked out over the factory complex, one of many that this truly multi-national company had scattered around the world. Behind him the door opened and he turned to greet the portly figure of Sir Charles Standish, as the company Chairman bustled in to shake the proffered hand. "Sit down, Mike, sit down", said Standish, and the two men sat at one end of the long boardroom table. "I hear the Brands test went well", continued Standish, taking a cigar from a box on the table and lighting up. "Yes", replied Brookes, "the chassis performed well, and while we had a misfire problem with the engine Alan Francis is pretty sure he can cure it".

"I know", confirmed Standish, "Harry Cooper has been keeping me abreast of developments there. He says they've got the problem pretty well licked".

"I must say", smiled Brookes, "that I wasn't at all sure about having Cooper around, but he's really gotten involved with the project".

"I know, it's infectious, get's the blood flowing in the veins more than any damn list of profit and loss can do". Standish tapped cigar ash into an ashtray and was silent for a few seconds. "Funny about Peter Snelgrove, though", he said eventually, "fancy him turning up. Did you invite him?"

"No. He wrote to me a while ago, but with everything else that was happening I never gave him a reply. He must have heard about the test and just turned up. I'm damn glad he did, though; he really showed what the car might be able to do. I'd ideally like him to drive for us at the Targa".

"Difficult politically, Mike, he has a reputation. I don't think my board would want to be associated with a driver who worked for the Nazis then sat the war out in Switzerland".

"Well, it's true that he drove for two teams that were the darlings of the Nazi government, but that's not the same thing as him working for the Nazis. Remember, he didn't come from a wealthy background so he had to go where the pay cheques were. In those circumstances I don't think I can blame him for grabbing the opportunity to drive for two of the best outfits in the world at the time. As to his sitting the war out in Switzerland it seems there's more to that than meets the eye, so I think I'll do a bit of digging and see what I can find out".

"Well", Standish replied cautiously, "I can't stop you doing that, but I should warn you that whatever you come up with had better be good if you want him to drive for you, otherwise the Lynx board will create all sorts of problems for the project, besides", continued the Lynx Chairman, changing tack, "he's a bit old for all that now, isn't he?"

"Bonetto was forty-nine when he won the Targa four years ago", responded Brookes, "and there's a guy called Fangio out there who's still winning Grands Prix. As to your other point, bad publicity's no good to me either, so you can be sure I'll keep you posted on what I find out".

"Fair enough, now what about the other drivers?" Brookes pursed his lips. "Well", he said, "I think Piers Furnley deserves another shot. He put in a number of consistent laps and if he can find a bit more speed he might work out pretty well".

"Rawnsley-Bysh?" queried Standish, and Brookes groaned.
"Oh I know you know the family and all that but he's a
bloody idiot, he's not right for the Targa, he'd just balls it
up somehow or other".

"You can't blame the boy for trying, Mike".

"I wouldn't blame him if that was why he went off. Any
racing driver worth his salt has to find his own limits and
those of the car he's driving, and that means sometimes
there are spins and accidents..."

"...exactly my point", interrupted Standish. "Charles",
continued Brookes, "Rawnsley-Bysh went off because he
felt Snelgrove had shown him up, which he did, but when
he found he couldn't match Snelgrove's pace he tried to
ignore the rev limit, the engine cut and he bent one of my
cars because he ignored my instructions. I don't want him
driving for me". Standish stood and walked to the open
window, still puffing the cigar. "Tell you what I'll do", he
said, "you give him another test and if he bends the car
again I'll pay for any damage out of my own pocket, how's
that?"

"What is it with you and this family?" asked Brookes
caustically, "Masons are you?" Standish smiled. "No", he
replied, "but his father is a very old friend of mine, his son
has his heart set on this drive and he has asked if I can
help, which I am happy to do as long as Adrian measures
up as a driver. How about it, Mike, give him another
chance, OK?" So saying Standish stepped to Brookes chair
and held out his hand. "Shake on it, one more chance and
if the boy doesn't measure up I'll say no more about it".
Brookes grimaced.

" 'The boy' as you call him is trouble, Charles", he said, but
he shook the proffered hand. "Good!" exclaimed Standish
and returned to his seat. "Now, Shoji Takamura". Brookes

gaze flicked skywards and back, "now what?" he asked. "Well he's definitely coming to London for one thing, and he wants to meet you for another".

"Oh? When did all this happen?"

"I had cause to speak to him on the 'phone and I mentioned how well the Brands test had gone. He sounds interested". So, now, was Brookes. "When will he be here?" he asked. "End of the week", replied Standish. "You're sure?" enquired Brookes. "I'm sure", confirmed Standish. "Can you set up a meeting?"

"I can. He'll be here for a week or so, when would suit you?"

"Just set up the meeting, I'll be there".

"I don't like it!" exclaimed Alan Francis bitterly. "Bloody Japs, I spent four years fighting those bastards in India and Burma and some of the things I saw will never leave me". Francis sat in the upstairs office opposite Brookes, who leaned forward, arms resting on his desk. "I fought them too", he said, "in the Fleet Air Arm I fought Italians, Japs and Germans, but the war's over, we have move on".

"You weren't on the ground", Francis continued, "you didn't see..." his voice trembled and the sentence trailed off. Francis stood and peered out of the window down to the factory floor below. "When will you meet him?" he asked. "I had hoped", replied Brookes, "that *we* would meet with Takamura in London the day after tomorrow".

"Not me", said the engineer, "if Takamura offers us a good enough deal I suppose you have to go for it, but it's going to take me a while to get used to the idea, if I ever do". Francis moved to the door and pulled it open, "let me know how you get on", he said, stepping through to the walkway and closing the door behind him. In the office Brookes ran a hand through his hair and watched as the engineer made his way to the stairs and stepped down to the floor below.

A noise at the side door attracted Brookes' attention and he glanced in that direction as Mark Spall entered. "Ah, Casanova", he said wryly and Spall grimaced. "Come on Mike", replied the Finance Director, "I've apologised for that, and Gina..."

"Is a cracker", interposed Brookes, "yes, I'd noticed..."

"I was going to say that Gina has promised not to print anything unless we clear it first".

"Gina is a journalist", Brookes replied, laying on the saccharine world-weariness a little heavily, "and will do what is best for Gina, now, what can I do for you?" Spall gave up trying to convince the boss and sat down. "Holland and Pendlebury..." he started. "Yes", Brookes interrupted, "good news?"

"Well, yes and no", continued Spall, "they're very interested in sponsoring us but want some proof that we can do the business before they commit big money to us. Makes sense, I suppose".

"What are they offering?"

"They'll give us five thousand pounds for the Targa. If we get a good result there, they'll sponsor us for a full World Sports Car Championship season, maybe two".

"What do they consider would be a good result?"

"A podium placing, top three". Brookes rubbed his eyes with the palms of his hands. "Apart from miracles", he asked, his hands dropping back to the desk, "what do they want for their five grand?"

"Pretty much what I mentioned before - including their *Palm Beach* brand in the name of the team, photo shoots before the race, and their Marketing Director wants to accompany the team to the Targa". Brookes smiled, "fancies a freebie to Sicily does he?" and Spall shrugged. "OK Mark", Brookes said, "well done for keeping them on the hook. I had hoped we'd get a lot more from them up-front, but that was probably a bit optimistic". Brookes tapped a finger on the desk, "still", he mused, "their proposal could have possibilities, but I'll have to think about it. When do they want a reply?"

"I can keep them on the boil for a while. How long do you need?"

"A lot will depend on what, if anything, I can get from Takamura. I'll give you a reply of some sort by the end of the week, how's that?"

"That shouldn't be a problem" said Spall, getting up to leave. As he reached the interconnecting door his companion called him and the Finance Director turned back. "I've been pretty involved with the racing programme recently", said Brookes, "how are we doing elsewhere?"

"Well, the Swift is still selling quite nicely and we've had some orders for the Seafire, but we don't have a lot of fat to live on if the going gets tough for any reason."

"And the bank manager?"

"Oh, he's fussing, but no more then usual".

"OK Mark, keep me up to date". Spall nodded and turned back to the door, when Brookes spoke again. "Mark, I'm sorry I got hot so hot under the collar about Gina d'Alessandro, but you do need to be careful about what company information you let her have, OK?"

"OK Mike" replied Spall and stepped through to his office.

9.

Early Summer was in full bloom and the train was hot and stuffy as it puffed and rattled its way into London. In the corridor-less slam-door compartment Mike Brookes sat by an open window and tried to concentrate on the copy of the Daily Express that he was reading, although his thoughts kept drifting to his impending meeting with Shoji Takamura. Glancing back at the front page of the newspaper he read again the headline article revealing that the United States had backtracked on its commitment to help finance Egypt's construction of the Aswan High Dam, and was likely to be followed in it's decision by Britain. Deeply paranoid over 'Reds under the bed' the U.S. Administration was evidently developing a nervous twitch concerning Egypt's burgeoning links with the Soviet Union. Britain had its own political problems with Egypt and appeared happy to tag along for the ride. Brookes had no time for overblown political posturing, regardless of its source, and was chiefly concerned with how all this fuss and feathers would affect the Middle Eastern oil supplies that were vital to the success of his business.

The suite at The Dorchester that the Japanese businessman had taken was plush in the extreme. In his mid fifties, with thick greying hair, it was Takamura himself who opened the door in answer to Brookes knock. Smiling broadly, the Japanese was dressed in regulation European business suit and was accompanied by an attractive young female interpreter dressed in more traditionally Japanese kimono. "Please come in Mister Brookes", she said , indicating one of several comfortable armchairs arranged around a coffee table. Brookes stepped through the door and shook hands with Takamura. "You will take tea with us?" asked the girl. Previously, the closest Brookes had been to a Japanese was tailing Zero's over the Pacific and Indian Oceans while trying to shoot them down, and on one or two exceptionally uncomfortable occasions having the situation reversed, however, he knew enough to appreciate that the Japanese prized polite formality highly, and accepted graciously.

Seated, Takamura spoke in deep guttural tones while the girl prepared tea and translated what was, essentially, small talk to which Brookes responded in kind. Finally, with all three seated, Takamura got down to business and spoke through his interpreter. "Mister Takamura", she said, "understands that your racing programme is proceeding and that the recent test at Brands Hatch went well".
"Yes", replied Brookes, "we had a few teething troubles, but..." The girl translated as he spoke, but now interrupted. "Teething troubles?" she asked, "I am not sure I understand..."
"Ah", said Brookes, appreciating that this could be a very long meeting, "babies, when they first grow teeth, cry a lot, but it's not a serious problem. When the teeth come through they are fine". Her face brightened, "oh yes, of course, silly of me, I should have guessed". Takamura spoke to her, she replied in rapid-fire Japanese, the businessman laughed and the girl blushed prettily. "Mister Takamura", she said, "finds it amusing that you should be teaching me about babies". Takamura spoke again and the girl interpreted. "Mister Takamura understands that you intend to enter your cars for the Sicilian Targa Florio in the Spring of next year, is that correct?" Brookes glanced at the businessman, nodded, and the Japanese continued.

"This race is of great interest to JTC", the girl translated, "it being long-distance and over difficult public roads, a good result would be excellent publicity". Brookes explained that his thinking coincided completely, the girl passed this on and Takamura smiled and lapsed into thought. With the Pegasus director on the point of breaking the lengthening silence with a comment of his own, Takamura spoke again. The interpreter listened and turned, "do you know how many pit stops you will need?" she asked. Brookes had done some preliminary work on this, and while he would need more information on petrol consumption over long distances, calculated that with a race distance of some ten laps of forty or so miles each, he would plan to bring the cars in twice, on laps three and six. This would also tie in with the regulations, which demanded that a driver do no more than five consecutive laps at any one time. All this he explained to the interpreter, who passed it on to Takamura. Again the businessman lapsed into thoughtful silence, before once again addressing the young interpreter. Turning to the Pegasus director, she said "Mister Takamura says that JTC can make for you a tyre specifically for the conditions that you will encounter in the Targa Florio. It will last for the three laps that you require".

For Mike Brookes it was now his turn to lapse into a thoughtful silence. On the face of it this was a golden opportunity, but there was much to consider. Eventually turning to the interpreter, he asked whether JTC had experience making tyres for this highest level of competition, and waited for Takamura's answer, which, as he suspected, was 'no'. However, the Japanese did confirm that JTC was in the process of recruiting technicians and experts from other companies who did have the necessary racing background. Brookes was perfectly well aware that for his team to be fully competitive he needed a factory backed tyre deal, and was also well aware that, as a new entrant into the motor racing arena himself, beggars could not be choosers. "What is Mister Takamura's proposal", he asked, "is he prepared to offer a tyre contract, and on what terms?" Aware that this was perhaps a little blunt, he nevertheless needed to know where he stood, and once again waited as businessman and interpreter went into a huddle before getting a reply that was not quite what he had anticipated. "Your company, Pegasus Cars", asked the interpreter, "is not quoted on the stock market, is it?" A little nonplussed, Brookes replied, "no, it's a little early in our development. Perhaps later".   With another few words exchanged between the Japanese, again the interpreter turned back. "Mister Takamura sees a big future for sports cars in Europe", she said, "and believes that the two companies could profit by closer cooperation.   Consequently he proposes to buy a one-third share in Pegasus Cars at a price to be agreed, the package to include a tyre contract for the Targa Florio and any other racing projects that you may wish to enter in the future".   'So here we go again', thought Brookes and wondered if perhaps the handiwork of Charles Standish might be detected in this anywhere. Standing, he walked to the window and looked down on a Park Lane bathed in warm summer sunshine, men in shirtsleeves, girls in bright print summer dresses. Once again he turned the prospect over in his mind, as he had done many times since Standish made his proposal on behalf of Lynx, and he came to the same conclusion – he was not yet ready to take on partners. Returning to the armchair he sat and passed the message back to Takamura. The Japanese nodded soberly. "Perhaps", he said haltingly, "we might discuss this again at a later date?"

"You speak English!" exclaimed Brookes. "A little", smiled the businessman "but Asuka", he said nodding in the direction of the girl, "is at university in England and speaks the language very much better than I, as you will have observed".

"So where do we go from here?" asked Brookes, and Takamura fell into renewed dialogue in Japanese with the interpreter, who then relayed the result of their conversation. "Mister Takamura", began the traditional opening, "is very interested in having his tyres showcased at the Targa Florio. He notes your connections with The Lynx Motor Company and believes that an entry in next year's race could achieve significant results. Consequently he is prepared to enter into a contract to supply tyres for your team". Brookes was exultant, but kept his feelings hidden pending the answer to his next question. "On what terms?" he asked. Takamura looked thoughtful and then spoke once more through the interpreter. "The JTC tyre", she said, "will be of a completely new type. Firstly, it will be tubeless..."

"Tubeless?" queried Brookes, "experience in racing with tubeless tyres is pretty thin on the ground. You don't see that many of them on road cars, although they are supposed to be safer..."

"Precisely so", commented Takamura in English, before motioning for the girl to continue. "In addition" she said, "the tread and construction of the tyre will be of a completely new radial design..."

"Radial?" interrupted Brookes, and Takamura spoke in Japanese to the interpreter. "Mister Takamura", she continued, "says that the new design will enable the tyre to have flexible sidewalls with a stiffened tread area. With more tread on the road, road holding will be much improved over traditional cross-ply designs". Brookes scratched his head, suspecting that he knew what was coming next. "These revolutionary tyres", he said, "I presume you want to develop them alongside my racing programme, using my cars and drivers as guinea pigs".

"Of course" Takamura replied in English, "testing of the tyres will take place in Japan to assess basic performance and safety issues, but Pegasus race cars will take that testing to its logical limits".

"What will it cost me?" the Pegasus director asked and Takamura switched again to reply through the interpreter. "JTC will supply tyres and the wheels to fit them, Pegasus will supply the cars and drivers on which to develop them. That seems to be an equitable partnership, no money need change hands". Once again, it seemed, as with the Lynx engine, that Pegasus was to be used as a test bed, but the principal of that company, sitting on the armchair in the plush suite at The Dorchester Hotel, did not really see how else he was going to get a tyre contract, and anyway, if they were as good as Takamura seemed to think... "I have to consult with Lynx and one or two others", Brookes replied, "but personally I would be in favour of giving your radials a try".

"Good enough", replied Takamura in English, "how long will you need?"

"Better say a week, will you still be here?"

"I must fly first to France and then to Germany, but I should be back here in seven days".

"Good enough", said Brookes.

With the 1956 Targa Florio, at the north-western tip of he island, completed in the Spring, top-level motor racing returned to Sicily in the summer for the Grand Prix at Syracuse, in the south-east. In 1955 the 3.4 mile circuit had been the scene of the first post-war major event win for a British car, the Connaught-Alta, piloted by a British driver, Tony Brooks.

Although not in the same league as its illustrious neighbour to the north, the Syracuse track, roughly triangular in shape, and fast, with average lap times in excess of 100 mph, was still a driver's circuit, requiring inch-perfect placing of the car lest a mistake pitch car and driver into the concrete wall bordering much of the lap distance. It was also the headquarters and principal test track for Scuderia Cordoba.

One year on from their début triumph, dark green British cars were nowhere in evidence at the front of the grid. Hungry for revenge, fiery red Italian machines occupied the front row, the Ferrari of Jorge Nalbandian snatching pole position marginally ahead of the Cordoba Maseratis of Mauro Falletti and Heinrich von Schmidt. As the flag dropped, the big front-engined single-seaters roared off the line and Falletti got the jump on Nalbandian, who tucked in behind the Maserati with von Schmidt's similar car close behind in third. For eight laps Falletti managed to fend off the hard-charging Nalbandian, but on the ninth lap, entering the sharp left-hand corner before the pits, the Italian left his braking just a little too late and slid off, the car's impact with the wall scattering debris across the track. Falletti emerged with nothing worse than cuts and bruises, but following him into the corner,

Nalbandian's Ferrari ran over debris and the front-right tyre blew. With the car slithering into the main straight, the Argentine grappled with the wheel as the Ferrari slewed from one side of the track to the other. Gaining control just in time, he drove slowly along the approach road to the team pit where the offending wheel was quickly changed, but the best part of two minutes were lost with the unexpected excursion, and Nalbandian re-entered the race at the back of the charging pack. Now, however, the Argentinean displayed all the skill for which he was rapidly becoming legendary and set off after the leaders. With six laps to go he had fought his way up to fourth place, with four laps to go, third, and with two laps to the chequered flag he lay second, wheel to wheel with von Schmidt's leading Maserati. The fervent race-mad crowd around the circuit cheered to the echo as Nalbandian tried everything he knew to get by but was blocked again and again by the German ace. Finally, approaching that self-same left hand corner before the pit straight for the last time, Nalbandian risked all by leaving his braking later and later. With the Ferrari snaking up alongside the Maserati, von Schmidt blinked first and braked. Catching the Ferrari in a tyre-smoking slide onto the straight, Nalbandian accelerated hard and crossed the line to take the win half a car's length ahead of the German driver.

Following the presentation, Nalbandian handed the large, bright, silver trophy cup to the tall, slim, tanned, trophy girlfriend and escorted both to his 'company car', a bright yellow road-going 3-litre Ferrari 250, through the post-race throng to an accompaniment of relentless 'click' 'clicking' press cameras that was, for the time being, music to the ears of both. Unusually, this was the girl that he had seen during his stopover in Sicily months previously, although, not so unusually, there had been other girls, at other race meetings, in other countries, in-between.

The drive back along the coast road to Palermo was exhilarating and Nalbandian drove quickly, both to impress the girl, as boys will, and because they were invited that evening to dine with Don Pietro Sevila y Cordoba at his villa in Bagheria.

The evening was warm and clear and Sicily basked beneath a star spangled sky as Jorge Nalbandian drove the growling Ferrari slowly along the driveway to the villa entrance, and came to a halt. As he and the girl stepped from the car, Don Pietro and the Cordoba team manager, Salvatore Castellotti, walked down the steps to greet them. "Jorge", said the Don with the studied informality that only the true aristocrat can muster, and held out a limp hand, which Nalbandian shook. "Don Pietro", he replied and then repeated the formality with Castellotti. Turning with not the slightest reluctance to the girl Don Pietro held out his hand, lifted hers to his lips and gave the hand the merest touch. The evening was informal and the men wore casual jackets with open-necked shirts. The girl, however, had no intention of being overlooked in what promised to be a testosterone dominated evening, and wore a long, dark, evening dress, the bust of which subtly accentuated her cleavage. "Signorina...?" asked Don Pietro, "Francesca d'Ursino", replied Nalbandian. "Charming, utterly charming", murmured the Don, who had all the appreciation of the Italian male for a beautiful woman. Offering the girl his arm, which she took, Don Pietro led the way into the villa.

Their meal that evening was served on an open veranda overlooking the Mediterranean. A warm summer breeze rustled the leaves of nearby trees as Don Pietro's chef served two Sicilian specialities, Zuppa di Fave, followed by Spaghetti alle Vongole, the latter made with clams caught that very afternoon. Dry white wine was consumed with the meal, and as the girl had suspected, the conversation included a generous helping of motor racing anecdotes. In honour of Nalbandian's great win at Syracuse that afternoon, and despite the fact that one of the Don's own cars was narrowly beaten into second place, to follow the meal, instead of liqueurs, Don Pietro produced a bottle of Moscato di Siracusa, the sweet, white, Sicilian wine from the Syracuse area so rare that it was generally believed to be extinct. Even Don Pietro's extensive cellar contained only this bottle and one other. As the wine was sipped with due deference, Don Pietro stood and motioned for Nalbandian to follow him out onto the veranda, where he stood the wine glass on a balustrade and gazed out over gently lapping waves of the Mediterranean.

The two men stood in silence for a time before Don Pietro turned to his companion. "Jorge", he said, "you are one of the finest young drivers of your time, quite possibly the equal of Moss". Nalbandian's ego was sufficiently well developed to accept any amount of flattery at face value, particularly from a motor racing grandee of the stature of Don Pietro, and he smiled graciously. "For how long", continued Don Pietro, "are you contracted to Ferrari?"
"For the remainder of this year, and all of nineteen-fifty-seven, Don Pietro".
"For Formula One?"

"Yes".

"And what of the Targa Florio?" asked the Don and again Nalbandian smiled, this time with anticipation. "Don Pietro", he replied, "of all the races in the world I would like to win the Targa, for I believe it to be the most difficult and dangerous, more so even than the Mille Miglia". This was music to the ears of Don Pietro, who felt exactly the same way. "Are you contracted to Ferrari for next year's Targa?" he asked. "That is difficult to say", replied Nalbandian, remembering the Commendatore's less than promising comments. "My contract does not specifically mention races other than Formula One, but it does not specifically allow me to drive for other teams in other disciplines either. It is rather a grey area, and of course I would be reluctant to cause troubles with the Ferrari team that might affect the rest of my career". Don Pietro took up his glass and sipped the wine. "Of course I know Enzo Ferrari very well", he smiled, "a cunning fox that one, he will play his cards very close to his chest". For a time there was silence save for the muted conversation of Francesca and Castellotti at the table, and the gentle lapping of the waves along the shore. "I will be frank", continued Don Pietro, "I want you to drive for me in the Targa Florio next year. As you may be aware it is the one major race in the world that my team has never won and even before the Grand Prix today I was convinced that you are the driver to give me that win. We will purchase for you the best cars, you will have virtually unlimited financial and technical backing. What do you say, Jorge?"

"It is a very tempting offer, Don Pietro, but first I must clear my path with Ferrari".

"Very well Jorge, discuss the matter with Signor Ferrari and let me know. If necessary I will talk to Enzo myself and we shall see what can be arranged". So saying Don Pietro took the young driver by the shoulder and they walked back to the table.

10

Mike Brookes read again the account of the Syracuse Grand Prix on the back page of the newspaper. It had been a superb drive by Nalbandian, and Brookes hoped that the young Argentinean would not drive in the next Targa, for he would be formidable opposition if he did. Down below, the factory hummed and clattered with the sound of cars being constructed, and reluctantly Brookes turned back to the lead article on the front page of the paper.

To replace the now defunct international finance package for the Aswan Dam, Egyptian President Nasser nationalised the Suez Canal Company, effectively taking control of the waterway and the substantial income gained from it. This completely unexpected move by the Egyptians caused consternation among maritime nations worldwide, but particularly to France, which originally constructed the canal, and Britain, as the colonial power responsible and with vital trade links to the Far East. Yet no ships were arrested, and the ships of no nation were excluded or threatened with exclusion from this economically vital conduit for international shipping. Nevertheless, stung by the unwelcome surprise, and with no love lost between himself and Nasser, Prime Minister Anthony Eden indulged in disturbingly hawkish rhetoric over what Britain intended to do about the seizure.

Brookes dropped the paper on his desk and stood, muttering under his breath his unflattering opinion of the world's politicians as a breed. Glancing at his watch he realised he needed to get a move on if he were to arrive on time for his meeting in London with George Stepanek, and picking up his jacket he headed out of the office.

Taking advantage of the good weather Brookes drove to London, threaded his way around the suburbs and finally parked across the road from the North London garage at which Stepanek worked as a mechanic. He glanced at his watch again, it was 12.30 – lunch time – just right. Brookes stepped out of the car and walked across the quiet tree-lined suburban thoroughfare with its large Victorian houses, to the garage, which stood on a corner with the main road. Stepanek came out to greet him and the two men shook hands. "Let me get out of these overalls", the mechanic said, "and I'll be right with you". Emerging a few moments later from the back of the garage, now attired in shirtsleeves and corduroys, Stepanek called out to the office, "Hey, Harry, I go to lunch now, OK?" A tousled head bobbed into view around the door, shouted, "OK George", bobbed back, and then bobbed out again, this time followed by it's owner, also the owner of the garage, a tall individual in his thirties. The new arrival swept a hand across his head and whistled appreciatively, "well", he said, admiring the Seafire parked across the road, "you don't see many of those about".
"Well, not yet perhaps", agreed Brookes. "Yours?" asked Harry, and the owner nodded. "Harry Morell", interjected Stepanek, "meet Mike Brookes, the owner of the Pegasus Car Company".

"No", said Harry, sticking out a hand, "really?"

"Really", replied Brookes, shaking the hand. "I'm always looking out for articles about you in the motoring press", continued Morell with enthusiasm, "you and Chapman".

"Oh yes, Colin Chapman", replied Brookes, "great designer".

"The both of you", said Morell, "and now the rumour is you're getting into motor racing like Lotus".

"Well, Harry, you know rumours..."

"Oh come on, you can tell me..."

"Right now", Brookes offered as diplomatically as he could, "I need a word with George here, OK?"

"Oh sure, sure. Hey!", exclaimed Morell suddenly, "I just thought, you're not going to poach him from me are you? He's a damn good mechanic you know".

"Yes I know, and no, nothing like that", replied Brookes not entirely truthfully, since one of his objectives today was to try to persuade Stepanek to sign on as Chief Mechanic for Team Pegasus, at least for the Targa. Brookes waved and the two men turned away, but Morell called out. "Hey, mind if I look over the car". "Not at all", responded the Pegasus director, turning back. Pulling the keys from a trouser pocket he tossed them to Morell, "take her for a spin around the block", he called, "but don't bend it, I've got to drive it home! OK?" Morell caught the keys. "Bloody right", he said, "thanks, I'll take good care of 'er, don't you worry".

"You just got a friend for life", said Stepanek with a grin, "all he talks about is sports cars and racing".

"Sounds like my kind of bloke. Now, where can we get a pie and a pint!?"

Walking a short distance they came to *The Battle of Waterloo,* a sizeable pub that Stepanek said also provided good lunches. Outside the hostelry hung a sign depicting Lady Butler's famous painting of the charge of the Royal Scot's Greys at the aforementioned battle, and inside a busy hum of lunchtime trade greeted the new arrivals. Brookes elbowed his way to the bar and ordered a pint of the dark brown Irish gold, Guinness, for Stepanek, and a pint of lager for himself. Making his way back with the drinks, he handed the Guinness to Stepanek, who then led the way to one side of the bar where a decent sized area was set apart with tables for diners. Having chosen a table by a window looking out on the busy street, they thirstily sampled their drinks and studied the menus. Having made their choices, Stepanek this time elbowed his way to the bar to order grilled plaice for himself, while Brookes indulged in a personal favourite, steak and kidney pie. The two men chatted casually of shoes and ships and motor racing until one of the many bar staff brought their meals to the table. The food was steaming hot and both plates were piled high with peas and the inevitable chips to accompany their main choice. A wicker basket of fresh bread rolls and a plate loaded with a number of small plastic containers of butter also arrived, and they were ready. "So, Mike", opened Stepanek as they tucked into the food, "how can I help you?"

"I have a problem", said Brookes, "I need a top class driver for the team, but all the Moss's and Nalbandians are already committed to others, and anyway being perfectly honest with you George, I doubt that I could afford them".

"But...?" offered Stepanek. "Yes", continued the younger man, "but. I watched Peter Snelgrove drive one of my cars at Brands Hatch and I think I caught a glimpse just how bloody good he must have been in his heyday". Brookes paused, unsure of how to proceed. "You would like him to drive for you at the Targa?" interjected Stepanek. "Damn right I would!" exclaimed Brookes, "and I want you as Chief Mechanic, but there are problems. I couldn't pay either of you top wages up front, I just don't have the money, and there's also the problem..."

"Of Peter's history".

"Exactly. It's not just my decision, you see, I have to convince Lynx and our sponsors that Peter Snelgrove will not bring bad publicity with him, because at the end of the day that's what everybody is in this for, me included if I'm honest. Oh, I love motor racing, no mistake about that, but I'm entering Pegasus in the Targa Florio to boost my company's image so that I can sell a lot more road cars".

"Yes I see".

"George, when we were down at Brands Hatch you hinted that there was more to Peter's war record than meets the eye. If there's something you know that will help, let's get it out in the open!" George Stepanek was quiet for some minutes before replying. "It is very difficult", he said finally, "for reasons both official and personal to Peter".

"Come on George", said Brookes, sensing that he might be on to something, and desperate to find a way to get both Snelgrove and Stepanek into the team, "don't go coy on me now. You suggested that I contact you. Well here I am, let's have it!"

"Mike, I am Polish, and of necessity we Poles are cautious about whom we trust. Nevertheless I sense that you are an honourable man so I will tell you, but whether Peter will thank me or drive for you once I have told you is another matter, and one that you will have to discuss with him".

"Fair enough", said Brookes. George Stepanek took a sip of the Guinness and, as they tucked into their lunches, began the story. "As you know", he said, "Peter drove for both Auto Union and Mercedes in the nineteen-thirties. I was race mechanic with him at both teams and I got to know him well". Stepanek drank again from the glass before continuing. "Things were difficult in Germany during the thirties, especially so for me as a Pole, but we spent much of our time outside the country, racing here and there and those times were still good. Winning was always good. Finally as 1939 dragged on, the Nazi rhetoric against my country increased dramatically and I was coming under suspicion, I felt sure that the Gestapo were following me. I could see the way things were going and so could Peter. He had friends at Maserati and arranged for me to join the team as a mechanic for the 1939 Targa. Peter lived in Germany at that time, knew the Germans and spoke German perfectly. Peter arranged for my immediate family to leave Krakow for Sicily, and once I got there with Maserati, we all caught a boat to France. Without Peter's help, and the assistance of his friends in Maserati, I don't know what would have happened to my wife and children. As it was my parents and many other relatives were killed in the war". Stepanek fell silent once more. "Quite a story, George", Brookes said quietly, "but I don't understand...?

"What happened to Peter and why he apparently spent the war in Switzerland?"

"Well, yes".

"I will tell you. As I said, Peter lived in Germany, had done for years. He knew the Germans, how they thought, how they carried on from day to day, and he spoke German like a native of the country..."

"So...?"

"So when Germany invaded Poland, September 1st 1939, Peter left for England to join up, but Government officials kept his application waiting, saying that they might have something special for him". Both men finished their meals as Stepanek continued. "In 1940 the Special Operations Executive was formed to infiltrate agents into occupied Europe, but not much was hoped for in Germany itself as the population was not generally against the Nazis, especially while they were winning, and anyway those that were against the regime went in fear of the Gestapo, which, in the years since Hitler came to power, had penetrated all levels and areas of society. Still, Georg Elser's failed attempt to assassinate Hitler in November 1939 showed that there must be some anti-Nazis somewhere, and Lieutenant Colonel Thornley, the head of the German and Austrian section of SOE, saw a chance to use Peter's special talents by recruiting him..."

"...and using him as an agent in Germany?" asked Brookes. "Exactly so", confirmed Stepanek. At this Brookes got up and returned to the bar, but since Stepanek had to return to work, and he had to drive home, this time he came back with only halves. Putting both half pint glasses on the table, he sat and took a drink. "OK George", said the younger man, "let's hear the rest of it".

"Yes, well, Peter was recruited for SOE with the intention of getting him back into Germany to contact dissident groups. Of course his face was well known in Germany, but with a moustache or a beard here, a change of hair style or colour there, it is surprising what changes can be effected, and anyway Peter was to stay well away from his old motor racing colleagues. As further cover, just in case he was recognised, the story was splashed across all the newspapers that he had declined to join the British armed forces and had absconded to neutral Switzerland".

"Yes", Brookes murmured, "I begin to see..."

"From his base in Switzerland, Peter covertly entered Germany on several occasions. Once he met von Stauffenberg..."

"The German officer who tried to blow Hitler up in 1944".

"Yes, but Peter met him some time before that, just after Stauffenberg had been wounded. He was a staff officer for the 6th Panzer Division and campaigned in Russia, you know"

"No I didn't know that".

"It was what Stauffenberg saw of German atrocities in Russia that turned him against the Nazis, but I gather that Peter did not get on with him".

"Oh", asked Brookes, by now fascinated with the unfolding story, "why not?" Stepanek smiled. "According to Peter", he said, "Stauffenberg may have been anti-Nazi but he was still a German officer, was rather arrogant and possessed of a good-sized ego. He was not aware that Peter was a British agent and Peter did not feel to disposed to reveal his identity, as Stauffenberg was a little too keen to advocate Communism in place of National Socialism. Peter, from his viewpoint, could see that there was essentially no difference between Stalin and Hitler".

"Was Peter involved in the 1944 plot?"

"No, he was not. It may have been better perhaps if he had been, for Stauffenberg and his co-conspirators were soldiers, fully aware of the consequences of their actions if they failed." Again Stepanek lapsed in silence, and Brookes waited until he felt able to continue. "No", Stepanek said finally, "Thornley got wind of the White Rose, and asked Peter to make contact".

"White Rose?" asked Brookes, "what was that?"

"White Rose", replied Stepanek, "was an anti-Nazi group started by a small number of students at Munich University, led by Sophie Scholl and her brother Hans".

"And Peter contacted them"?

"Yes", Stepanek confirmed, and his voice grew sad, "Peter contacted them and I believe became very fond of Sophie. You know, before the war Peter had been a celebrity. For the first time in his life he had money, and with all the glamour of motor racing he had the most beautiful and sophisticated women in the world at his finger tips, and he took maximum advantage of both opportunities. But it was Sophie, a pretty little 21 year-old student and some-time kindergarten teacher who stole his heart. Whether their friendship was anything more than platonic as far as she was concerned, I don't know, but I doubt it, she had a young man in the army, fighting on the eastern front. I think the fact that it was all so one-sided makes Peter's grief all the worse".

"What happened?"

"Sophie and the White Rose were innocents adrift in a sea of hate. They believed they could bring down the Nazi regime by peaceful means, by student means, painting slogans on buildings, distributing leaflets, that kind of thing. They had no idea what implacable enemies they were making. I believe Peter tried to dissuade them from doing what they were doing, but they were adamant. Innocent they may have been but they were not short of courage. Finally a Nazi party member saw Sophie and her brother throwing leaflets from a third floor window of the university to the courtyard below. Days later they were arrested, put on trial, found guilty and within hours executed, guillotined".

"Peter must have taken that badly".

"It broke his heart", Stepanek replied, "he blamed himself for not helping them, but what could he do? From their arrest to execution was two days, no more, and without help how could he take on the Gestapo? Some time later Peter made contact with Else Gebel, who had shared Sophie's cell on that final day. Peter told me her last words".

"What did she say?" Brookes asked, and, visibly moved, Stepanek continued. "According to Gebel, she said, 'It is such a sunny day, and I have to go. But how many have to die on the battlefield in these days, how many young, promising lives...'" Stepanek stopped, unable to go on. "Pretty, brave little Sophie", he whispered at last, "unwittingly she broke Peter's heart. He never married and I have never seen him with a woman since". Brookes was silent for some moments and then spoke again. "But this story", he said, "is nothing to be ashamed of, there's no reason why he should be shunned. Why does he not just put the record straight?"

"He cannot", Stepanek said, regaining his composure, "he signed the Official Secrets Act when he joined SOE. He is still bound by its provisions and can give no account of his activities without Government permission, and they will not give permission. Germany is now an ally in the fight against the new enemy, Communism, and it is deemed politically unacceptable to rake over old bones... If Peter tells his story he will be arrested and put in prison for many years". Brookes leaned back in his chair, "bollocks!" he said, and Stepanek smiled, "exactly so", he agreed. Outside London clattered on while inside the pub customers chattered on, and then Brookes had the germ of an idea. "But wait a minute", he said, leaning forward, "wait just a minute, there may be a way to get Peter's story out there without his appearing to have anything to do with it".

"How?"

"Never mind for the moment, just contact him and make sure he's in agreement. I want him to drive for me, I don't want to piss him off!" Again Stepanek smiled. "Yes I will ask him", he said "Peter wants a chance to drive again, I know this. I will ask him and I will contact you".

The shadows of summer stretched long into Autumn and Pegasus was a hive of activity. As the Motor Show approached Alan Francis perfected the flexible manifold, which cured the misfire. Inevitably, other problems arose and were dealt with, and a second test day came and went at Brands Hatch. Both Furnley and Rawnsley-Bysh drove again, together with a promising French driver, Charles Boulet. Freed of the misfire restriction both British drivers worked their way down to just under what Snelgrove had managed with the restriction. Brookes was encouraged by Furnley's progress but was still not sure about Rawnsley-Bysh, or was it, he wondered, just that he did not take to the young aristocrat? If that was all it was he would get over it. Boulet also showed good promise, although, it being his first outing in the car he was a little slower than his fellow drivers.

Of Gina d'Alessandro there was no sign, and when Brookes enquired after her whereabouts Mark Spall, still smarting from his upbraiding by the boss, replied a little defensively that she had gone back to Italy to process her story, but would return to the UK in a month or so. Brookes himself went into overdrive in an attempt to get everything in place in time, and having persuaded Lynx to accept JTC radial tyres, signed a tyre contract with Takamura, who advised that the first batch of tyres would arrive in September for track testing. With that problem solved, Brookes also accepted the Holland & Pendlebury sponsorship deal, and it was agreed that the new arrivals on the racing scene would be unveiled as *Team Palm Beach Pegasus Lynx* at the Motor Show. As a bonus Mark Spall managed to squeeze a little extra funding from Castrol in return for a couple of small decals on the cars and an undertaking to use Castrol oils - with attendant publicity potential if the team was successful. Still, money was tight and it was going to be a squeeze getting cars, mechanics, drivers, tools, spares, equipment, and tyres, ready and out to Sicily. A long journey by car and transporter lorry across the Alps in the Spring beckoned.

On a bright, warm, autumn morning the first batch of JTC radials were unloaded at London docks, passed through import formalities, loaded aboard a lorry and, accompanied by two JTC tyre technicians who flew into Heathrow from Tokyo the day previously, arrived at the Pegasus factory late that same afternoon. Fortunately the two Japanese spoke reasonably good English, but, just in case, Takamura gave Brookes the telephone number of the interpreter that he had used on his trip to Europe.

The following day, tyres, both the new radials and older cross-plys, a race car, mechanics and engineers climbed aboard a convoy of cars and lorries and made their way once again to Brands Hatch, where Brookes intended to test tyres and car to their limit by running them over a Targa race distance of some eight hours at racing speeds. Brookes himself would drive, together with Piers Furnley, and also invited to the trial for his specialised racing knowledge was George Stepanek.

In pit lane preparations got under way for the first stint, for which cross-ply tyres were fitted to act as a control and comparison base for the radials. The two Japanese technicians showed great interest and enthusiasm for everything concerned with the preparation of the cars, and Brookes was concerned and not a little annoyed to see Alan Francis being offhand to the point of rudeness with them. Finally the Pegasus boss took Francis out to the back of the garage where they could clear the air, and, while Francis simmered, told him in terms that he could not fail to understand that what was required of them all was the success of the team, and if that meant Francis being civil to the Japanese then that was precisely what Brookes expected to happen. The engineer appeared to accept the point and thereafter, while scarcely overflowing with fraternal bonhomie, did at least make some effort to be affable.

Brookes took the car out first, and with conditions dry and fine and no rev restrictions beyond the design maximum, was soon getting down to the 45.5 seconds that Snelgrove managed with the 18,000 rpm limit.   Within a couple of laps he was below that time and thereafter consistently lapped at around 40 seconds. After an hour Brookes brought the car back to the pits and had the wheels changed for those with radial tyres.   Charlie, Freddie, and the crew worked as they would have to in order to change tyres and refuel the car during a race, and the time was much too slow, but it was their first attempt. Brookes took the car out again and immediately noticed a significant increase in grip as the low, flat, profile of the new tyres gripped the road. Taking things steadily at first he built up speed bit by bit, but as racing speeds were approached, noticed that highly unpleasant tingling sensation, that feeling at the base of the spine that warns a racing driver that his temperamental mount is not behaving as it should. On cross-ply tyres Brookes took Paddock Bend very quickly, and hoped for better with the radials, but entering the corner for the first time in anger on the new tyres the car unexpectedly understeered dramatically, and with an ear-piercing screeching of rubber, slewed to the outside of the track and was bouncing across the grass perimeter before he regained control. Bringing the car back to the pits, checks were begun on tyres and suspension for the source of the problem, although Brookes suspected the radials as the car itself behaved well up to that point.

The pit crew ran through the gamut of problems that might cause the handling problem – suspension geometry, roll bar settings, balance weights - and each time Brookes tried the car again, at racing speeds the dramatic understeer reappeared. As work went on around the car, Stepanek engaged the two Japanese technicians in lengthy conversation, and finally approached Brookes. "Any luck?" he asked, and with Brookes shake of the head, continued, "think it might be the tyres?"

"It's looking very much like it. The question is, what happens to them at racing speeds that causes the problem".

"I've been speaking to the Japanese and I think I might have some idea", said Stepanek, and outlined his theory. "To allow the tread to sit squarely on the road to give the extra grip, the sidewalls of the tyres are flexible. I think that at present they are too flexible for racing speeds. They do not hold the car on a true line through the corner but allow centrifugal force to shift the weight of the car outwards. It is probably only a matter of millimetres but it is enough to upset the handling. If I am correct JTC will have to redesign them with strengthened sidewalls". Brookes groaned, "how the hell long will that take!?" he exclaimed, and called the two Japanese over. Following a long discussion, during which the limits of the technicians English became frustratingly apparent, the consensus of opinion was that the problem was tyre design and that JTC would have to go back to the drawing board. To their credit the Japanese were keen as mustard to help and the senior technician proposed returning immediately to Japan with one of the current batch of tyres in order to see how the problem could best be solved.

Brookes carried on with the schedule, and with cross-plys reinstated and Furnley driving, much valuable data was obtained over many hours relentless testing at racing speeds; for this was the unglamorous side of motor racing, the ceaseless search for improvements that might make a car fractions of a second per lap quicker in a race. As Furnley pounded round for lap after lap Brookes, Francis, Charlie, and Freddie, got their heads together and began to develop a system for pit stops, which Brookes based on his experience at Le Mans. Each man in the pit crew was to have his own job and be trained to perfect pitch for that job. Finally Furnley was called in, Brookes took over the driving and thereafter every hour, on the hour, brought the car in for a racing pit stop. At first the crew's attempts were shambolic, but with Furnley also pitching in with his experience of long distance sports-car racing, slowly some sort of order grew out of the chaos, although more, much more, training would be needed.

11.

For Mike Brookes and Pegasus, October 1956 started well enough. Shoji Takamura had his technical staff hard at work on a redesign of the tyres and was hopeful that a new batch might be ready before the end of the year. Hearing of Pegasus involvement in the Motor Show he also offered to contribute to the costs in return for a mention for JTC on the stand. This came as a considerable relief to both Brookes and Alan Francis who were struggling to meet expenditure, even with the stand, which necessarily was not small, in the accessories section of the show.

The JTC inclusion, while welcome, threw design of the stand into some confusion and the Japanese company's advertising representatives were the cause of much short temper, nail biting, and grey hairs, arriving as they did on the day before the Show's press launch to install a large company logo on the rear wall of the stand, which now represented the main partners in the racing venture arranged with the Pegasus and Alan Francis Engineering logos situated over the Lynx, JTC, and Holland & Pendlebury's *Palm Beach* logo's, stretched across the wall from left to right below.

Beneath the logos, and leaning at an angle against the wall to display the interior, stood a full size replica of the Seafire racer, resplendent in dark British racing green livery, with the team name in gold lettering along the sides, below the two-seater cockpit. Castrol decals occupied sections of the front bodywork behind the wheels. Brookes intended playing his cards close to his chest for a while yet, and the Seafire, strictly a mock-up, gave no indication to inquisitive spectators of the spaceframe design, weight of the car, or power of the engine. In front of the Seafire, on the floor of the stand and laid out in kit form, with body panels in matching racing green, was a Swift road car.

Brookes was pleased with the stand and the location, which, thanks to a little gentle persuasion applied to the organisers by Sir Charles Standish, was on the ground floor of the exhibition at the rear of the main hall that included all the major motor manufacturers, including Lynx themselves.

Press day was hectic and Brookes spent several hours on the stand fielding questions about the race car, (which generated a pleasing amount of attention), as diplomatically as he could. The Pegasus boss had signed Piers Furnley for the team and the driver was also on hand, showing an easy charm and self-deprecating humour in dealing with the press. Consequently, when Alan Francis turned up for his stint in the firing line, Brookes took time off to wander around and see the Show for himself, taking in the big new Jaguar MkVIII and, closer to his own field, a brace of new two-seaters, the Daimler drophead, and the MG Magnette. Always interested in innovation, the Pegasus director paid particular attention to the Rover T3 gas turbine powered car, and the Buick Centurion with its remote control steering.

Arriving at the Lynx stand, Brookes found Standish in attendance and the two shook hands. As befitted the largest British motor manufacturer their offering was impressive, boasting two top of the range saloons, and also en example of the Monaco family run-about. Brookes and Francis had found time to offer a few initial suggestions to Lynx to sharpen up the car's image and performance and Brookes was pleased to note that their ideas had been taken onboard and that from early in the new year Lynx would be offering a limited edition Sport version of the car, boasting twin SU carburettors for increased performance and upgraded suspension for better road holding. Both Pegasus and Alan Francis Engineering were prominently featured in the Sport brochure, and to tie-in with the racing programme the initial batch would be delivered in two-tone British racing green and white.

Threading his way back through the throng of journalists and invited guests, Mike Brookes approached the Pegasus stand, and even from the back and despite the fact that she was dressed in coat and slacks, the Pegasus boss recognised her as he approached. "Miss d'Alessandro", he said, "I wondered if you might be here".
"Mister Brookes", she purred, turning, "how nice to see you again".
"Does Mark know you're here?"
"I do not think so, I only flew in to London yesterday. Does Mark come to Earls Court today?"
"Not today. We'll all do a stint at the Show, but Mark will be here later in the week".
"Well, I will call him. Mister Brookes, perhaps I might arrange an interview with you this week some time?"
"That's possible, there is something I would like to discuss with you, although I can't promise you too much detail concerning the racing programme. I intend keeping that to myself for a little while longer, I'm sure you understand?".
"Yes, I see, but you do intend to enter the Targa Florio in the Spring, that is correct?"

"Yes, that is correct. Give me a call at the office and we'll set up that interview".

"Very well, Mister Brookes, I will call you". Brookes stepped past the journalist and returned to the stand. "Hi Alan", he called to the engineer, "everything OK?"

"Seems so, we've had a lot of visitors, plenty of people interested in the racing programme".

"Well keep it vague for the time being".

"Sure. Was that the lovely Gina d'Alessandro you were chatting to?"

"Yes, she wants an interview".

"Lucky bastard!" Brookes raised a quizzical eyebrow and turned to see the Italian journalist walk back through the crowd, and as she did so a man emerged from the throng and fell in step with her. "That's funny", said Francis. "What's funny?" asked Brookes. "The bloke that just tagged on to Gina", mused the engineer, "he was here earlier, nosing around the racer and asking all sorts of questions".

"Which you answered with due circumspection?"

"Oh, played strictly with a straight bat old boy! Blocked every one!"

"Did he say who he was?"

"No, but he's a Mediterranean type and knows his racing cars. From his questions I would guess he's an engineer of some sort".

"OK, let me know if he turns up again".

Show days were long and tiring, and on the evening following one such day, Mike Brookes arrived home in Essex looking forward to a scotch on the rocks and an early night. Calling out as he turned his key in the lock, he heard Nicola reply from upstairs and heard her coming down as he turned into the lounge and made for the drinks cabinet. "How was it?" she asked, entering the room behind him. "Long", he said, "but pretty good. We're picking up orders for the Swift and we've had a few for the Seafire as well. At this rate the Show might even pay for itself". She put her arms around him and gave him a quick kiss. "Have you eaten?" she asked. "Yes", he replied, "grabbed a bite at Earls Court before I caught the train. Drink?" She nodded and walked through to the kitchen to retrieve a number of ice cubes from the refrigerator, bringing them back in a saucer. Dropping two each into two tumblers, Brookes poured a gin and tonic for Nicola and a scotch for himself. Turning on the small black-and-white television in the corner, Brookes sat beside Nicola and waited for the set to warm up. Picture and sound eventually arrived to display the headlines on the late evening news, headlines that confirmed what had been evident all day. The war of words with and over Egypt grew more strident with every passing hour, and Brookes got up once more turn the set off. "I just can't believe that Eden would do anything stupid", Nicola said as he returned to the sofa "That's what I used to think", he replied, "but all this bloody sabre rattling is getting a bit out of hand". Snuggling together the two sipped their drinks. "Fancy going to bed?" she asked. "Mmm", he murmured, "but only to sleep, unfortunately".

"I can see", she teased, "that when we go to Sicily, I'll have to get myself an Italian stud".

"You bloody dare... " The harsh ringing of the telephone interrupted and Brookes got wearily to his feet. "Now, who the bloody hell...?" he asked stepping to the jangling instrument and picking up the receiver. "Hello?" he asked, and a voice babbled quietly at the other end of the line.

"What!?" barked the Pegasus boss, "speak up, I can... Hello? Freddie? Is that you? Where are you? ... Brookes paused and listened. "OK, be careful I'm on my way now!" So saying he slammed down the receiver and turned to Nicola, sitting bolt upright and wondering what all the fuss was about. "That was Freddie Kendal", he said, "he and Charlie are taking a turn looking after the factory".

"I thought they were working for Alan in Walthamstow?"

"They are but this is Wednesday, he always closes at mid day today because he's open all day Saturday. Freddie and Charlie have been doing the same, so they said they'd take a turn looking after the factory. We've all been taking turns, it was my stint tomorrow".

"And when were you going to break that piece of good news to me?" she enquired archly. "Tomorrow", he said. "Look, you can bend my ear about it later, right now I have to get to the factory, they think there's someone creeping around in there. Where are my car keys?"

"Leave the Seafire", she said, "they'll hear it coming miles away at this time of night. The Wyvern is outside, we'll go in that".

"We?" He asked, "you're not going". Getting up from the sofa, she slipped on her shoes, picked up her handbag, opened it and removed the keys to the Vauxhall. "I'll drive", she said, "do you want to stand here arguing about it or do you want to get going?"

"Oh bloody hell!" he exclaimed, knowing full well that she would not be dissuaded, "come on then, let's go!"

In the darkened factory, Freddie quietly replaced the receiver on to the telephone in the receptionist's office, and turned to face the stairway to the upper level. Charlie stood by the stairway and tiptoed back to Freddie. "Get him?" he asked. "Yeah", was the reply, "he's on his way. What's happening?"

"Well there's definitely someone up there in the boss's office. I can see a torchlight and hear movement".

"We going up there?" asked Freddie. "We could wait here I s'ppose", whispered his companion, "this is the only way out, but we don't know what whoever is up there might find. We better go up. OK?"

"OK". Charlie turned back to the stairs and slowly began to ascend, followed closely by Freddie. Reaching the top, and with the walkway stretching before them, both could see the torchlight beam moving back and forth in the office at the far end. Slowly and carefully both tiptoed along the walkway until, after what seemed like hours, they arrived at the door, which was ajar. Carefully, Charlie reached inside, felt around for the switch, and turned on the light.

Turning into the lane that ran past the factory gates, Brookes told Nicola to pull up. Along the right hand side of the lane trees and undergrowth flourished, and along the left side a grass bank and shrubbery fronted the fence that skirted the factory. As was usually the case at night, the light over the gates, which were open, was on, but the car park and the factory complex itself were in darkness. Brookes stepped out of the Wyvern, bade Nicola stay where she was, made his way to the factory gates and peered inside. In shadows at the far end of the car park, close to the factory, Brookes made out the old van that Charlie and Freddie used for their chimney-sweeping sideline, but could not see any other vehicles. Then, peering around to his left, in dark shadow, he saw the open-topped two-seater sports car. A figure sat in the driver's seat, attention fixed on the factory, and Brookes quietly stepped around the gate, out of the light, and towards the car. Leaning over, he grasped the ignition keys and pulled them out of the dashboard. Startled, the driver turned towards him. "Well, Miss d'Alessandro", he said conversationally, "I thought our appointment was for Friday. Bit early aren't you?" The journalist glared at him in silence, and he smiled. "If looks could kill", he said, "OK, let's find out what you're doing here, shall we?"

The man was tall, balding, in his late thirties, and of olive-skinned Mediterranean appearance. "OK", barked Charlie, "who the hell are you?" His reply was a shrug. "Listen buster", Charlie continued, "we've got you bang to rights, breaking and entering, so let's have it, let's have some I.D." The man appeared to consider his position, then slowly reached into an inside pocket, lifted out what looked like a passport and tossed it over. Passing Charlie's shoulder, it fell to the walkway and Freddie knelt to pick it up. Quickly their 'prisoner' leapt forward and barged into Charlie, who fell backwards over the kneeling Freddie. Jumping over the tangled twosome, the intruder ran along the walkway to the stairs as Charlie and Freddie struggled to their feet to give chase.

Brookes heard the commotion and saw a dark figure burst from the factory and make for the sports car, followed by two others. The first of the trio saw the unexpected and unwelcome new arrival at the car, changed direction and ran out of the gate.

Sitting in the Wyvern, Nicola heard the rumpus and was in the process of opening the door in response, when she saw a figure run out of the gate and turn towards her,

136

followed by the familiar figures of Charlie Small and Freddie Kendal. With the car door ajar, she swivelled around in the driver's seat, leaned her elbows back on the passenger seat, raised her knees, and as the first of the charging trio reached the car, gave the door a hefty kick with both feet. The door shot open with considerable force, to be rapidly succeeded by a loud 'thump' and a shout of pain and surprise. With their quarry floored, Charlie and Freddie piled in and dragged him to his feet. "Well played", said Charlie in admiration as Nicola stepped out of the car. "Bent the door a bit, mind", he continued. "Not to worry, we'll get a replacement from a breaker's, be good as new in no time. "Now, you", he said, turning his attention to the intruder, "let's try again, shall we?"
"I think you break my nose", was the mournfully nasal response.

The office was crowded. Nicola sat behind Brookes desk, while Gina d'Alessandro occupied the only other chair, muttering to herself in staccato Italian. Brookes, Charlie, and Freddie kept watch on the intruder. "What's she on about?" asked the Pegasus boss, indicating Gina. "She appears", responded Nicola, "to be casting doubts upon your parentage, and the parentage of all your ancestors back to the dawn of time".
"Yes! Yes!" exclaimed Gina, waving an angry hand in his direction, "bastardo!" Brookes smiled and turned back to the others. "Now", he said, "do we know who Raffles here, is?" Freddie Kendal fished in a pocket. "We asked him for some I.D.", he said, "and he threw this to us. We thought it was a passport, but it seems to be a pocketbook of some sort". Kendal handed over the book, and Brookes glanced through it. "The writing looks as if it might be Italian, can

137

you make head or tail of it?" he asked, dropping it on the desk in front of Nicola; and picking it up, she flicked through the pages. "It appears", she said, "to belong to Engineer Carlo Franconi. This", she continued, indicating the intruder, "is presumably Engineer Franconi".

"Yes I think I've seen him before", pondered the Pegasus boss, "at the Motor Show. Alan Francis said he had been snooping around the stand, and later we saw him with Mata Hari here". Gina d'Alessandro threw up her hands in frustration, "idiota!" she exclaimed at her partner in crime, and Brookes addressed the journalist. "Not very good at this cloak-and-dagger lark, are you?" he said. "Perhaps you should have done what you do best and tried getting the information you want lying on your back". D'Alessandro turned angrily away, and Brookes resumed his conversation with Nicola. "Anything useful?" he asked. "Some Italian telephone numbers", she replied, "shall I try one?"

"Why not?" Brookes confirmed. Picking up the telephone, Nicola asked the Post Office operator for a number, and hung up the receiver. The lines were not busy at that time of night, and the call quickly came through. Nicola picked up the receiver, "pronto", she said, then exchanged a few words in Italian before hanging up the receiver. "There's nobody there", she said, and glanced at her watch, "well, it is past midnight in Italy. But the operator tells me that the number is for the headquarters of the Cordoba racing team in Syracuse".

"Cordoba", mused Brookes, "well, it's nice to know they consider us worth spying on..."

"You propose to enter the Targa Florio", interrupted Engineer Franconi, still nasal and dabbling his bleeding nose with a handkerchief. "Don Pietro pays close attention to all entrants for that race. It is the only major event that his team has never won. For him, as a Sicilian, it is of major importance". D'Alessandro suddenly snapped at him in Italian and a sharp exchange took place. "Thieves falling out", Nicola commented with a wry smile. "Charlie, Freddie", said Brookes, "take Franconi downstairs and keep him there while I put a proposition to d'Alessandro. Nicola, I'll need you to make sure she understands in both languages. OK?"

"OK boss", the two mechanics replied in unison, and propelled the engineer through the open door and along the walkway. "Now", continued Brookes, addressing the smouldering journalist, "we have you and your colleague, as we say here, 'bang to rights', breaking and entering and industrial espionage". D'Alessandro looked away, fully aware of her predicament, but the Pegasus boss spelled it out anyway. "We can ruin you Gina", he said, "completely destroy your credibility and reputation. If we hand you over to the police you will be tried, convicted, and serve a prison sentence, plus, Franconi's involvement and our testimony will drag the hitherto good name of Cordoba Racing through the mud. Correct?" The journalist made no response and Nicola prompted her in her own language. "Yes!" the Italian snapped, "alright! What do you want!?"

"That's better", continued Brookes, "now, here's what I want you to do".

The Motor Show ended 27th October with Pegasus on the crest of a wave. Orders for the Swift and Seafire road cars were dramatically improved, and both specialist magazines and the sports correspondents of the national dailies were hungry for as much information as they could get on the company's entry into motor racing, speculation over the likely driver line-up being particularly rife, with some very high-profile names being bandied about. Brookes enjoyed the publicity and would dearly have liked some of those mentioned to drive his cars, but, while Pegasus' fortunes appeared to be improving, it was still a long way from being able to attract that kind of talent, although he did nurture hopes for a competitive outing in Sicily.   It was two whole days before the euphoric bubble burst.

29th October dawned cool and clear in Essex, but with storm clouds over a Middle East on the verge of war. An incursion by Israeli soldiers into Egypt resulted in a series of sharp, hard-fought actions with units of the Egyptian army. All this was part of a plan, initially devised by the French Government, but backed to the hilt by Britain, intended to provoke a crisis that would provide an excuse for an invasion of Egypt in the area of the Suez Canal by substantial units of the British and French armed forces, on the pretext of keeping the Canal, a vital international trade route, open. Invading troops were soon heavily engaged with the Egyptians and the Canal turned almost overnight into a war zone, triggering a turn of events completely the opposite of those anticipated. Tankers from Middle Eastern oil fields were forced to take the long trip around the Cape of Good Hope to Europe, adding the best part of a month to the journey time and forcing the price to skyrocket while Britain's oil supplies dwindled rapidly away..   U.S. President Eisenhower, piqued that Britain and France should take such action without American approval, and doubly miffed since he was currently heavily involved in a campaign for re-election, refused to allow exports of U.S. oil to Britain and France unless those countries agreed to withdraw their troops from Egypt, sonorously declaring that military force was not the way to settle international disputes, (unless, of course, it was U.S military force, when presumably it was perfectly acceptable).

Mike Brookes watched these cavortings on the political stage with jaundiced eye and no little concern for the future of Pegasus as the new orders, hard-won at the Motor Show, suffered a rash of cancellations as petrol supplies dried-up, long queues formed at petrol stations, and the price rocketed to six shillings per gallon. For his part, Mark Spall had his mind taken off the ramifications of the Gina d'Alessandro affair by a series of grillings on the telephone from an increasingly alarmed bank manager.

As the news from abroad got steadily worse, Britain and France came in for increasing worldwide condemnation for their actions, and with the British economy apparently teetering on a precipice, Mike Brookes and Mark Spall were summoned to their branch of the Midland Bank in person. It was not without some trepidation that they entered the building, with its sedate oak panelled interior, to ask at reception for the manager.

Eric La Grange was tall, slightly stooped, with receding grey hair swept back from his forehead. Now in his late fifties he was from a well-to-do family, and his straight laced wife would have been shocked to learn that, as a youth in the nineteen twenties, he seriously considered setting off for Paris and the left-bank, there to become a great painter. His father, however, sternly forbade any such foolishness - public school and banking had been good enough for him and for his father, and so it would be for young Eric. Now, despite his long, long, years in banking, La Grange still displayed the slightly uncertain air of someone who really should be somewhere else and was doing this merely to fill in until somebody who liked all this number-crunching came along and he could be off to pastures new, pastures that, in his heart-of-hearts, he knew now that he would never see.

The receptionist showed Brookes and Spall into the manager's office, similarly oak-panelled to display prudent rock-solid dependency to customers, and Eric La Grange stood up behind his similarly portentous desk, leaned forward, shook hands with the new arrivals, waved them to the chairs opposite and resumed his seat. As he sat, Brookes glanced at the manager's blotting pad and noticed that La Grange had been doodling what looked very much like a passable representation of the Pegasus factory, which, as effective holder of the purse strings, the manager had cause to visit once or twice. La Grange was Spall's old boss and the two exchanged pleasantries and small-talk for a few moments before the manager got down to business. "Now, gentlemen", he opened hesitantly, "I have called you here because we really must do something about your overdraft, which is becoming somewhat alarming, and I, well, I really am afraid I cannot allow it to continue unabated".

"Mister La Grange", Brookes opened, mustering as much confidence as he could, "we have every reason to believe that as soon as this Suez fiasco blows over we can bring the business back on an even keel". La Grange ran a hand through his hair, "well, yes", he replied, "possibly, but how long will this Suez business go on. We have to do something now, Mister Brookes, the bank really cannot continue financing you to the extent that it is".

"What would you have us do?" asked Spall, and La Grange tapped a long finger on the blotting pad doodle on his desk. "Can you inject any capital of your own into the business?" he asked, "or could you offer the bank any additional security?" Brookes and Spall glanced at each other. "Well," said Spall, "you already have the mortgage on the factory premises, that's an extensive piece of real estate".

"Yes, yes, Mark, but if the economy tips into recession and we have to foreclose, could we sell it, and if so for what price? This is the sort of calculation that I have to make, you see. I know it's not very palatable to you, with the considerable effort that you must all have put into the business, but, well, I have to think of these things..."

"Foreclose?" Brookes cut in sharply, "you are thinking of foreclosing?"

"Mister Brookes", La Grange continued in the same hesitant manner, "I have to do what is best for the bank. If you can offer additional security...?" Again the two Pegasus directors exchanged glances. "The only other assets we have", said Spall reluctantly, "are the house that Mike Brookes lives in, and my flat. They both have mortgages, but the bank could take second mortgages..." La Grange stood and looked out of the window to the street outside. "Second mortgages", he murmured, "second mortgages. Very tricky, very difficult, I am afraid we would need more than that". He pursed his lips and tapped a long finger against them for what seemed like hours, until Mike Brookes broke the deafening silence. "My father", he said, "has a property in Preston, Lancashire, I don't think it has any mortgages attached". La Grange turned. "Would he agree to the bank taking a mortgage on it?" he asked. "I don't know", replied Brookes, "I need to talk it over with him".

"You know, of course..." started La Grange.

"...That he will lose it if the business goes belly up? Yes I know", Brookes responded concernedly, "and I'll tell him exactly that. It will be his decision".

"Well gentlemen, perhaps that..." started the manager. "How long can you give us", cut in Spall. "Well, no more than a week", responded La Grange, turning back from the window. "If you can let me know that your father is agreeable within one week, and if I give my personal recommendation, I think I can persuade the bank not to foreclose".

"Will you give your recommendation?" asked Brookes, and La Grange glanced down at the doodle on his desk. "You must love what you do" he said quietly, "to be willing to risk so much to see it through".

"Yes, I do, but..." La Grange turned once more to look out of the window. "It must be a fine thing", he murmured, "to have the courage and determination to follow your dreams, a fine thing indeed. Yes I will give my recommendation". The bank manager continued to gaze out of the window as his two visitors left.

For Mike Brookes, the long drive up to Lancashire was one that he made with extreme reluctance. For Alan Francis, Mark Spall, and himself to gamble everything on the business was one thing, but if his father should put his home in hock to the bank and lose it, that was quite another; and yet, try as he might to rack his brains for some other form of security, he could think of none. Everything else the partners had, including Francis' workshop in Walthamstow, was already mortgaged past the roof.

Brookes parked the Seafire outside the terraced house, walked to the door and knocked. Presently he heard noises inside and the door opened to reveal his father. "Hello Michael,", the older man said, "come in, come in", and Brookes stepped into the hallway. The two men exchanged pleasantries and Arthur led the way through to the small but tidy kitchen while he made them both a cup of tea. "So", he said, "your enquiry after Peter Snelgrove when you were here last wasn't just idle speculation?"

"No", confirmed Mike with a smile, "he wrote to me asking for a test drive, although I have to say that what with everything else that was going on, I forgot all about him until he turned up at Brands uninvited".

"And?"

"You know damn well, Dad, he was bloody impressive".

"He hasn't lost his touch, then. Will he drive for you at the Targa?"

"Hope so. We'll have to do another test at Brands early in the new year. Full race distance, we'll decide the final driver line-up after that". Arthur handed his son a cup of hot, sweet, tea, and led the way back into the lounge sipping his own similar brew. "But you won't drive yourself?" he asked, seating himself in his preferred armchair, while Mike sat himself on the settee. "The plan's still the same", replied the younger man, "I have put my name forward as a reserve driver so that I can put in some test laps, see how the cars are handling, that sort of thing, but I don't anticipate driving in the race".

"Pity, you're a pretty fair racer yourself. You and Snelgrove would make a hell of a pairing".

"Can't see it happening, dad, much as I'd like to drive, I'll have too much to do keeping the team on the ball in the pits". The two men sat in silence for a time, sipping the hot drinks. "So", said Arthur eventually, "what brought you all the way up here at such short notice? Must be important, and probably not good news, so let's have it". Mike took a deep breath. "The bank is after us", he said. "What with this Suez business we've lost a lot of orders and the overdraft is growing like Topsy".

"Suez!" exclaimed Arthur, "I wouldn't have believed Eden could be such a bloody fool!"

"No, me either, anyway the bank wants a cash injection or more security and they want it quick".

"Or?"

"Or", Mike continued, "the manager says they'll foreclose". Again the two men sat in silence, and again it was Arthur who broke it. "How long have they given you?" he asked. "A week", replied Mike. "Generous of them", countered his father with heavy irony, "do you have more cash or security?"

"No, I don't." Arthur Brookes stood and looked out of the window at the small, neat front lawn, edged with his pride and joy, the rose bushes just beginning to burst with the new season's growth. He sipped his tea. "We could offer them this house", he said finally. Mike stood, "look, Dad..." he said, pained at having to ask, but desperate to save the business. "I know", Arthur said, waving a hand, "I might lose it. But if we don't put it into the pot you will lose the business and all those years of hard work, just when you might be about to turn the corner. When this Suez nonsense blows over you'll get things back on track.

146

Anyway, you're my son, of course you must use the house as security. Let me have the forms and I'll sign them as soon as you like".

"Dad, you'll never know how grateful I am for this. If there's ever anything I can do...?"

"Well there is one thing".

"Name it!"

"I'd really like to meet Peter Snelgrove!"

Around the turn of the year, in an attempt to bring some sort of order to the chaos, the British Government introduced petrol rationing, and down in deepest Walthamstow Charlie and Freddie abandoned their chequered second careers as chimney sweeps in favour of getting in on the ground floor of the brief demand for 'Suez Specials'. The boys began scouring the area for clapped out cars which they then bought at knock-down prices and, with the old 'bangers' ensconced on the bomb-site opposite the workshop, offering them for sale at an attractive mark-up, the demand being not for the cars but their logbooks, each additional logbook entitling the owner to an extra petrol ration. Proceeds - not spectacular, but handy nevertheless - were split three ways with Alan Francis.

Finally, in the face of worldwide condemnation, Britain and France were obliged to begin preparations to withdraw unconditionally from Egypt, oil supplies began to ease somewhat, and by early 1957, with a number of the lost orders regained, Mike Brookes and Pegasus were gearing up for the Targa Florio in the Spring.

For some time a drip, drip of stories had appeared in various European newspapers and periodicals concerning a well-known but unnamed former racing driver who had been engaged in espionage work against the Nazis during World War II, these stories being largely drowned by the deluge of dramatic events firstly in Egypt, and subsequently Hungary, which felt the heavy tread of Russian army boots in its streets. Finally, as the tumult died away, the Daily Express broke the story that unconfirmed reports named the mysterious driver as Peter Snelgrove, who, contrary to popular belief had not slunk away to Switzerland for the duration, but had in fact been based there by SOE in order to carry out subversive operations in Germany. Mr. Snelgrove, the article concluded, was not prepared to comment. In this era of the developing Cold War with Russia, cloak-and-dagger stories were particularly fashionable and the revelations caused quite a stir.

The noise of activity coming up from the workshop below was reassuring, and Mike Brookes smiled to himself as he replaced the newspaper on the desk. Gina d'Alessandro had done her work well, the story was out and in accordance with Snelgrove's express wishes, the White Rose affair was not mentioned. The telephone rang, Brookes picked up the handset and recognised the voice at the other end of the line. "Peter", he said, "seen the papers?"
"Yes", replied the driver, "it's bloody amazing, I've already had two team managers on the 'phone offering me testing contracts".
"And?"
"I said I'd drive for you, Mike, and I meant it".
"Good. I have another race distance test booked at Brands for Saturday week".

"I'll be there". The two men were silent for a while. "Well", Brookes said finally, "not long now".

"No".

"Think you can take the young bucks you'll be up against?"

"We'll just have to see, won't we?"

"See you at Brands, Peter". Brookes hung up, and Jeanine immediately put through another call. "Charles", Brookes greeted the Lynx Chairman, "good to hear from you".

"Read the papers, Mike?" asked the older man. "Certainly", confirmed Brookes, "anything in particular you had in mind?"

"This Snelgrove business, you wouldn't have had a hand in that would you?"

"Me? What could I possibly have to do with that? Anyway it's good news all around, we get a driver who's not only first rate, he's a bloody war hero. The publicity we can get from this is enormous, and It's started already. I havn't told Snelgrove yet, but as soon as Holland & Pendlebury heard that he could be driving for us they started pestering the life out of Mark Spall to persuade him to pose with the car for one of their photo shoots".

"Well, let's hope he can still drive, particularly for hours at a time, as I said before, he's not a young man any more".

"And as I said before, tell that to Fangio, he seems to be doing all right!"

"What are the chances of there being two Fangio's?" asked the Lynx Chairman pointedly. "Well", replied Brookes, "Peter will join us for a race-distance test at Brands shortly, which will give us a better idea. But to answer your question directly I can only repeat what the man himself said, we'll just have to wait and see, won't we?"

149

12.

Test day at Brands Hatch dawned misty, but with a forecast for early summer sun in prospect for the first time in it's short existence *Team Palm Beach Pegasus Lynx* gathered en masse and in good spirits. Two lorries transported a racer each, the Wyvern and the Austin Chummy transported mechanics and engineers, and a caravan of cars arrived bearing executives from Lynx and Holland & Pendlebury. JTC had delivered an improved batch of tyres so the two Japanese technicians were in attendance, as was Shoji Takamura, who flew in from Japan especially for the test.

Mike Brookes was adamant that only those directly involved would be allowed in pit lane, and arranged for the use of the enclosed glass-panelled visitors box opposite the start-finish line, where hot drinks and sandwiches were served for any onlookers, which today also included the press - the publicity surrounding the unveiling of Pegasus racer at the Motor Show and the subsequent revelations concerning Peter Snelgrove making it impossible to keep this test a secret.

Carefully and painstakingly mechanics and engineers carried out final checks on the cars, while the drivers, dressed for the first time in British racing green team overalls courtesy of Holland & Pendlebury, chatted amongst themselves. Similar overalls for pit crew were promised for the Targa.

In the first garage a racer stood, bonnet raised, while Alan Francis listened carefully as a mechanic in the driver's seat gunned the big V8 motor. Francis motioned for the mechanic to drop the revs and the engine note dropped back to an expectedly 'lumpy' tickover - thoroughbred racing engines were never happy at slow revs. Francis motioned for the mechanic to switch off and the engine stopped. Between them Francis and George Stepanek, in his new capacity as Chief Mechanic, were welding the pit crew into a well run, well-organised unit, Stepanek's experience with the formidably efficient Mercedes and Auto Union teams proving invaluable. Now the Polish engineer stepped into the garage and engaged Francis in deep conversation as they went over the myriad details to be attended to for the cars to run at maximum efficiency. Hearing movement and conversation behind him, Francis turned to find Shoji Takamura, accompanied by the pretty kimono-clad interpreter, in conversation with his tyre technicians at the rear of the garage. Turning, Takamura approached Francis and held out his hand. "Mister Francis", the Japanese said in his halting English, "I am very pleased to meet you at last". Francis stood immobile, his gaze stony, and made no attempt to shake the proffered hand, which slowly dropped back. "I understand, Mister Francis", continued Takamura, "that you were in Burma during the war". Struggling to retain his composure, Alan Francis replied with an icy "yes, I spent four years in India and Burma and saw things out there, things that your army did, that will never leave me". Slowly Takamura put an arm around the girl's slim shoulder, "Asuka", he said, "my daughter as well my interpreter and now my only child. My eldest son was, like Mister Brookes, a navy pilot, but he did not return from the Coral Sea". Takamura paused for a few seconds then wiped a hand across his brow. Asuka gripped the hand around her shoulders with her own and Francis remained silent.

"Might I ask, Mister Francis", continued Takamura, "what branch of the service you were in?"

"Royal Engineers".

"Ah yes, of course, highly appropriate. Did your unit by any chance participate in the attack on Meiktila?"

"In 1945? Yes we were with 7th Division, IV Corps".

"Then you will remember the Irrawaddy crossing in early February of that year?"

"Yes", snapped Francis, irritated, "what of it!"

"My youngest son was, like you, in the army, and was one of the defenders at that crossing. You remember the Allied air attacks, and the napalm that they dropped?" Francis bit his lip as the memories suddenly flooded back, the aircraft screaming in wave after wave to drop their lethal cargoes, the thick oily black smoke billowing back across the fast-flowing river, and the pungent smell of burning flesh. Most of all he remembered the exultation felt by himself and many others in his unit as Japanese soldiers across the river burned alive. Long ago he ceased to have any such feelings, but in the heat of battle in that bloody awful war... "My son died in those attacks", continued Takamura, and paused before continuing, "I still have many sleepless nights thinking of how both my beautiful sons died, and the terrible war for which their lives were given. I do not make excuses for them or for myself, but surely it is true to say that no nation that engages in war emerges with clean hands. We may never be friends Mister Francis, because of what we have been through, but let us at least try to be colleagues". Again Takamura held out his hand. Looking deep into the older man's eyes, Alan Francis found nothing save a deep sadness to match his own. This time he shook the offered hand, and without speaking turned back to the car.

Outside, as summer sunshine began to burn away the mist, Mike Brookes called the team - drivers, mechanics, and engineers - together. "In less than one week", he told them, "Italy will host the 1957 Mille Miglia, and one month thereafter, on Sunday 9th June, the race for which we have spent so much time and effort preparing, the Targa Florio, will take place in Sicily. I cannot stress enough how important it is that we obtain a good result in Sicily, a very good result. So now, let's get on with this test, shake out any last minute problems, and make sure that we are on that starting grid in great shape and ready to knock seven bells out of the opposition!" A cheer and a ripple of applause greeted his exhortation, and the team dispersed to its allotted tasks.

Brookes tried out the driver pairings that he intended to use at the Targa – Snelgrove with Furnley, and Rawnsley-Bysh with the Frenchman Charles Boulet.
Furnley and Boulet led off for the first two-hour session in their respective racers, while Nicola took the first stint timing them from the pit wall. Brookes sought out Shoji Takamura and went over again the prospects for the redesigned tyres. Using his halting English the Japanese explained that the new batch of tyres with the strengthened side walls should cure the handling problems, and that, in addition, they had been specifically designed with the Sicilian race in mind. "They will", explained Takamura slowly, "give maximum road holding characteristics for three laps of the Targa, approximately two hours of racing, but after that, due to the difficult nature of the mountain terrain to be encountered, performance will drop away rapidly, so you must make

absolutely clear to your drivers that they must do no more than their allotted laps between pit stops".

"That should be no problem", responded Brookes, "as you know we're geared up for pit stops every three laps". The Japanese nodded, "good, good", he said, "that was of course a prime consideration in our design calculations. We have tested the tyres in Japan, and they will be given a thorough workout today, but they are still a design very new to racing so we must not take unnecessary risks".

The first two hours of the test went according to plan with Furnley and Boulet swapping fastest laps and getting down to some very reasonable times around the Kent circuit. As was scheduled to happen in the race proper, the pit stops were staggered, with Furnley coming in first, followed by Boulet on the next lap. Brookes was on hand to supervise the stops with their refuelling, wheel and driver changes. Snelgrove immediately began to show his class, his lap times dropping dramatically, and with the cars now on different parts of the circuit as a result of the pit stops, something of a 'pursuit' developed, with Snelgrove inexorably catching Rawnsley-Bysh lap by lap, while the younger driver tried everything he could to stay ahead, his driving, much to Brookes annoyance, becoming increasingly ragged in the process.

With the first round of pit stops over, Mike Brookes waited until the track was clear then sprinted across and stepped up to the visitors box. The sun now dispensed noticeable warmth and many of the journalists and guests were outside and making use of the seats in the adjacent stands. Brookes made a point of chatting to the Holland & Pendlebury party, who seemed to be enjoying their day out from the office, and moved on to Sir Charles Standish. "Beats me why you are so keen to have junior drive for us", he said, jerking a thumb over his shoulder as a screech of tyres indicated a last-ditch attempt by Rawnsley-Bysh to stop himself being lapped by Snelgrove, which he failed to do. "He's a competitor", responded Standish, "that's what you need in a driver".

"What I need", replied Brookes, "is a driver who will compete with the opposition, not become obsessed with beating another driver in the same team". Standish smiled, "aren't you becoming a little obsessed yourself?" he asked. "Look at his times Mike, they are comparable with Furnley and Boulet, perhaps even a little faster. Let him get on with the job, he'll be OK on the day".

"I hope you're right, Charles, but he worries me." Beyond Sir Charles Standish, at the entrance to the visitors centre, Brookes caught a glimpse of movement and the swish of long auburn hair. Moving past the Lynx Chairman, he stepped through into the centre and recognised a familiar figure in trademark expensively casual slacks and blouse, with jacket slung carelessly across her shoulders. "Gina", he said, "so you came after all". The stunning Italian journalist swung around to face him. "Of course", she said, "I want to see for myself how the team performs".

"And?"

"Not bad, but you have no chance at the Targa, Jorge Nalbandian for one will see to that".

"Is he definitely entered?"

"I understand that Commendatore Ferrari will enter two cars for the race and that Nalbandian will co-drive one of them". This was news to Brookes, and not very welcome news. "Nalbandian is young and very, very, fast", continued the Italian triumphantly, flushed with remembrance of her humiliation at the hands of the English car maker. "Snelgrove is a has-been", she said, waving a deprecatory hand in the direction of the track, "and your other drivers are inexperienced boys. They will be no problem, you will be beaten and I shall have great pleasure in writing the story of your defeat". Brookes put on his best easy charm, knowing it would irritate her even more, "I thought you'd want Cordoba to win", he said, smiling. "Just as long as you lose", she said, turned and flounced away. Brookes watched her go and got that same stirring in his groin. 'Damn the woman!', he thought, annoyed with himself.

The day passed for the most part successfully, save for one or two glitches in pit-stop technique which were revealed and overcome. Late in the afternoon, Peter Snelgrove, George Stepanek and Alan Francis approached Brookes in the pits as he oversaw the crew packing up to leave. "Mike", Francis opened, "Peter noticed something during the last few laps of his final stint."
"Oh? Asked the Pegasus boss, "what was that?"
"Difficult to describe accurately", mused the driver, "the car just felt different, not as positive in the corners. Just different".
"Any of the other drivers notice anything?"
"No, Mike", responded Francis, "just Peter. Could be the tyres again of course, but I would suggest that we take the cars back, strip them down and give them a good check over".
"Good idea", said Brookes, "let me know if you come up with anything". Turning to Snelgrove, Brookes slapped the driver on the shoulder. "You were pretty damn quick out there", he said, "feeling confident for the race?"

"Looking forward to it", Snelgrove responded. "Peter has been training", Stepanek interjected, "getting himself fit".

"Well, you'll need to be at your best", the Pegasus director replied, "I heard today that Nalbandian will definitely drive for Ferrari".

"He's good", mused Snelgrove, "taking him on will be a challenge".

"You'll get the measure of him I'm sure!" Brookes exclaimed cheerfully, then clapping hands together, "OK boys, it's been a good day so I'm off to find Nicola, then we can track down a suitable hostelry and treat ourselves to a small libation or two!"

In the days following the test, Alan Francis and his team of engineers and mechanics went over the cars in detail but by the middle of the week found nothing that might contribute to the, admittedly minor, handling issues that Peter Snelgrove reported toward the end of the Brands test session. Brookes was nevertheless determined to get to the bottom of the problem, and with the cars rebuilt, decided to take one of the racers out into the Essex countryside to give it a work-out around twisting country lanes. Accompanied by Francis and two mechanics in the Wyvern, Brookes drove the racer to a quiet, zigzagging, undulating, section of road that he knew, and proceeded to blast the car up and down the road for an hour or more, finally pulling up behind the parked Wyvern. Alan Francis walked to the racer and leaned over. "Well?" he asked. "He's right", responded Brookes, "it's not handling uniformly. Sometimes understeer, sometimes oversteer. It's almost..." Brookes voice trailed off in thought. "Yes", prompted Francis. "It's almost as if the chassis is flexing", responded Brookes, "and it shouldn't be doing that to any appreciable degree".

"OK", said Francis, straightening, "we'd better get it back and strip it down to the frame".

It was Friday morning when the telephone rang in Brookes office and he picked it up. "You'd better get down here", said Francis, I think we've found something". Brookes hung up and trotted quickly down to the area where the racer had been stripped down. Alan Francis waited for him. "Here", he said, without preamble, and knelt beside the nearside front wheel area of the spaceframe skeleton. Brookes knelt beside the engineer and asked what he was looking for. "Here", repeated Francis, "where the tubing for the spaceframe is welded to support the suspension. The tubing seems to be holding up but small cracks are beginning to appear in the welds. Brookes lay on his back, ran fingers carefully over welded joints and felt rather than saw cracks in several of them. "It's the same with all four wheel arches", explained Francis as the Pegasus boss sat up. "Bollocks!" he swore, "so the chassis *is* flexing".

"Yes", confirmed Francis, "the power and 'G' forces encountered during cornering are too much for the welds. We're going to have to have them all strengthened".

"We've got a month to the race!" exploded Brookes, "how the bloody hell are we going to get all that done, get the cars rebuilt and out to Sicily in a month!"

"These welds will never stand up to the pounding they're going to get at the Targa", Francis said matter-of-factly, "they'll break up. The cars will be death traps". Brookes sat with elbows on raised knees and head in hands for several minutes. "OK", he said finally, "I'll get on to the sub-contractors straight away and see if they can fit us in, and if they can't help I'll keep trying until I find someone who can", then getting quickly to his feet he hurried back to the office and began telephoning.

It was late in the evening when Nicola heard the front door of their home open and close again. Coming downstairs she stepped into the lounge to find her fiancé slumped in an armchair, eyes closed. "Bad day?" she asked. Mike Brookes slowly opened tired eyes and looked toward her. "Terrible", he replied, and the eyes closed again. "What happened?" she asked, sitting on the settee. Brookes opened his eyes again, stood and walked to the settee and lay down with his head in her lap and feet on the armrest. "The handling problem that Peter noticed towards the end of the Brands test session..."
"Yes", she said. "...Well we found the cause", he continued, "welds in the spaceframe around the suspension mountings are starting to crack from a combination of the power being put through the wheels and the 'G' forces encountered during cornering. They will all have to be strengthened".
"How long will it take?" she asked. "Too long", was the tired reply. "The Mille Miglia is in two days time, the Targa a month after that, and the sub-contractors who originally fabricated the spaceframes are booked solid for two months ahead at least. I've spent all day trying to find an alternative".
"No luck?"
"No. Everybody seems to be up their ears in work, but I'll go in tomorrow and try again".
"You won't find many engineering firms open on Saturday", she said thoughtfully. "No", he said, "but I

have to try". Gently she stoked his hair as he put an arm over his eyes and tried desperately to think of a way out of this disastrous turn of events. The racing programme, his brain-child, had blossomed beyond anything originally countenanced, and now nothing less than the survival of Pegasus hung on the company competing in, and getting a good result at, the Targa Florio. With the likes of Lynx, Holland and Pendlebury, JTC and others onboard and raring to go, a no-show would destroy any credibility that he might have as a designer, and with that would go any future for Pegasus as a builder of road or race cars. For the first time Mike Brookes truly appreciated to what extent he was Pegasus, and just how make-or-break his reputation as an innovator in car design was to the company. The realisation did little to lift his mood as he contemplated potentially fruitless days ahead looking for a company able to quickly and efficiently cure the problem of the welds. The cost of the exercise did not escape his attention either. Even with time to do the work, Pegasus limited finances would be stretched to the limit and as a rush job the cost would certainly be significantly higher.

Sunday evening drew down with Mike Brookes in his office at the factory, no closer to a resolution of the problem and racking his brains for anybody that he had not yet tried who might undertake the work. The telephone rang and he slammed his fists on the desk in frustration. Snatching up the handset he snapped an angry response. "Mike", said Mark Spall, "have you heard the news?"
"News!? What bloody news!?" Brookes replied irritably.
"It's all over the radio and TV bulletins, there's been a

crash during the Mille Miglia", said Spall, "a bad one, there's all hell to pay!"

"Tell me!" exclaimed Brookes, wondering what else could possibly go wrong, "calm down and tell me what happened!"

"The Marchese de Portago crashed his Ferrari Testa Rossa near Brescia, killed himself, his co-driver, and nine spectators..."

"Bloody hell fire!"

"...The Italians have gone ballistic, they're talking about an immediate ban on all road races, and that includes the Targa!"

"*What!*?" Brookes yelled down the 'phone.

At the Brookes home, Nicola sat nervously drumming fingers on the arm of a chair while Brookes paced up and down the room, and then, not for the first time that evening the jangling telephone cut through the palpable tension. Nicola picked up, listened, spoke a few words in Italian and replaced the receiver. "That was the Italian operator", she said, turning to Brookes, "they still can't get through, the line to Vincenzo Florio is still engaged".

"Did you keep the call in?" he asked. "It's midnight now", she said, glancing at her watch, "and Italy is ahead of us. They'll try again early in the morning. Signor Florio seems to have been on the telephone for hours, so I don't think he will thank us for waking him in the small hours; and you too need to get some sleep, you've barely rested for days. You need to be sharp and think clearly, and If you carry on like this you'll be useless for anything". Brookes massaged the knotted nerves at the back of his neck and knew she was right, but held grave doubts that sleep would come. Nevertheless he allowed himself to be propelled towards the bedroom and they lay restlessly together. Finally abandoning any hope that he might sleep, Nicola turned to another time-honoured method for taking their minds off their problems, and for a time the world contained nothing but their physical and emotional love. Too soon dawn's light crept over the windowsill, and close behind marched the new day, dragging all its intractable problems behind it..

Between the parlous state of the telephone lines to Italy and the fact that Vincenzo Florio was beset from all sides with urgent questions as to the fate of his famous race, it was days before Nicola, with Brookes in attendance, finally managed to get through to the Sicilian. What he had to say was not encouraging as both the mainland Italian and the Sicilian authorities seemed bent on banning all future road races. Florio himself seemed saddened and surprised by the realisation that a number of high-profile individuals who had for years basked in the reflected glory that the race brought to Sicily in terms of status and tourism, quickly turned their backs on him and were now baying for it's cancellation. Knowing what he did of politicians, Brookes was not at all surprised.

Vincenzo Florio was no longer a young man, but he was still a fighter, and he concluded the call by informing Nicola that while the race would almost certainly not take place in June, he was determined that it would be staged later in the year. Brookes hoped he was right for the team's whole effort was built around the Targa. Now nearly half-way through the year, there was quite simply not another race that could take its place in terms of stature and publicity, and with finance already desperately short, he wondered seriously if Pegasus would be around at all in 1958.

The next few weeks were hellish for the Pegasus boss as he fielded worried calls from Sir Charles Standish, Holland and Pendlebury, and JTC, while trying to sort out the problems with the chassis, news of which was kept firmly in-house, both Brookes and Alan Francis going to great lengths to ensure that Harold Cooper, Lynx man at Pegasus, was kept out of the loop. In fact the delay, (presuming that it turned out to be only a delay and not a cancellation), in the running of the race gave much needed time in which to work on the problem, and following a series of searching discussions with the original sub-contractors, Brookes arranged for them to take in the two chassis that he intended to race in Sicily, their instructions being to substantially strengthen *all* the welds, not just those around the wheel arches. Cooper was spun a yarn that the team were using the extra time to give the chassis a final check over and seemed happy with that.

Days turned to weeks as Brookes continued to field agitated calls from all and sundry, while becoming equally agitated himself during Nicola's many calls to Italy. For months the Italian authorities steadfastly refused to countenance the running of any road races, but finally were persuaded to allow the Targa Florio to take place on Sunday 27th October.

Nicola replaced the receiver and gave Brookes the news. "Bloody hell", he said, running a hand through his hair, "thank God it's back on, but the end of October. I wonder what the weather will be like?"

"Same as everywhere else in Europe at that time I suppose", she said quietly, "chances are that it will be wet. I'm pleased for you that the race is on, but I'm even more pleased that you won't be driving. The end of October's late in the year to be racing 300 horsepower brutes around the Madonie mountains".

"To say nothing of conducting a couple of transporter lorries and carloads of mechanics over the Alps", he said reflectively.

South of Palermo, at the villa in Bagheria, Salvatore Castellotti followed the manservant, who the Scuderia Cordoba team manager felt certain had been chosen by Don Pietro partly for his imperious manner. As he ascended the marble staircase he felt again familiar butterflies in the stomach as he was ushered into the presence of Don Pietro. On hearing his team manager announced the Sicilian nobleman turned from his balcony, and, to Castelloti's surprise and relief, smiled a smile as warm as the late summer breeze that drifted in from the Mediterranean. "Castellotti!" exclaimed the Don, and to his team manager's further surprise, stepped forward and held out a limp hand, which Castellotti shook. "My dear Castellotti", enthused the nobleman, "you have heard the good news, of course?"

"That the Targa Florio has been reinstated?"

"Yes, yes", bubbled the Don, "the race will take place after all. Vincenzo Florio has been able to convince those fools that on no account should this race be cancelled for something that, after all, happened elsewhere".

"I understand", responded Castellotti carefully, "that Signor Florio may have had some assistance from yourself in this matter?" Don Pietro tapped the side of his nose conspiratorially, "in strictest confidence, yes", he confirmed. "Florio is a great man", the nobleman continued, "and his race an enduring tribute to his genius, but he is not politically minded. Fortunately, I am".

"Is Signor Florio aware that you were instrumental in having the race reinstated?" asked Castellotti, taking advantage of his master's good humour. "No, he is not! And I do not wish him to find out!" snapped the Don, before continuing. "I know those damned politicos in Palermo, I have had many dealings with them and I know...oh...what is that Anglo phrase..." the nobleman snapped his fingers impatiently as he hunted for the words. "Where the bodies are buried?" offered Castellotti disingenuously. "Exactly so, Salvatore, exactly so!" confirmed the nobleman. It was, after all, a singularly apt phrase, Castellotti considered, bearing in mind that a number of the 'politicos' referred to by the Don were undoubtedly sponsored by the Mafia.

"Can you believe it!" the nobleman growled, "they actually tried to insist that the race be run at the end of November, and be for little street cars only, not my beautiful racers! Well, my dear Castellotti, this year I shall not be denied! The race will be open to all, as usual, and Scuderia Cordoba will win the Targa Florio!"

"Let us hope so, Don Pietro..."

"Hope!?" bellowed the Don, "hope has nothing to do with it! We *shall* win. I have spoken with Commendatore Ferrari, he will not enter a works team for the race this year, but has agreed to our purchasing two factory-specification Testa Rossa's and he will loan Jorge Nalbandian to us to drive in the race! What of 'hope' now, Signor Castellotti!?" finished the nobleman with a triumphant flourish. "With the combination of Nalbandian and the Testa Rossa's..." smiled Castellotti, being swept along with the Don's enthusiasm. "Exactly so!" enthused Don Pietro, "We have the best driver and the best car in the world, we must win! Who is to deny us this victory!?"

"Well", said Castellotti, aware that he was about to step onto thin ice, "I believe that Pegasus..."

"Those shoestring garagistes!", exploded Don Pietro, "beginners! They have no chance!"

"Engineer Franconi..." began the team manager. "That fool!" snapped the nobleman "he and that wretched d'Alessandro woman almost cost us our reputation!"

"Quite so", continued Castellotti, "nevertheless Franconi is an excellent engineer and he did acquire a few details of the Pegasus racer before they were discovered. He is of the opinion that it will be a very competitive car".

"Rubbish!" snapped the Don angrily, "the man is a fool! Their car is unproven, and in any event, who do they have driving for them? A has-been and a few inexperienced no-hopers. They will fail!"

"Of course, Don Pietro, they will fail", responded Castellotti, acquiescent on the surface at least, but nevertheless determined that Scuderia Cordoba would have cars and drivers at their maximum peak of efficiency for the Targa Florio.

13

Alan Francis looked aghast. "Bloody hell", he said with feeling, "is that the best we can do?" Standing beside him in the Pegasus factory car park, Mike Brookes scratched the back of his neck, looked a little bemused, and nodded. "No budget", he replied, also with feeling. The objects of their attention were two large but elderly AEC coaches that the team had purchased with the intention of ripping out the insides and converting them to transporters, one for the two racers and one for as much spare equipment as could possibly be hauled to Sicily. "Hells bloody bells", continued Francis, expressing the feelings of both men, "it's going to be a frigging nightmare getting those bastards across the Alps! Is the whole team going in those!?"

"Racers, spares, mechanics, just about everything but the drivers, who we can just about afford to fly out. Can't have them knackered before we start". Francis groaned. "There is some good news, though", continued the Pegasus boss. "Oh goody, do tell", said Francis, heavy on the irony. "Well", responded Brookes, "on the odd occasions that I did convoy duty up in the Arctic during the late unpleasantness, I noticed that the convoys would often as not take tugs with them to help ships that got into trouble and pick up survivors. On the same principle we've also bought that..." Francis looked at the direction in which Brookes pointed and beheld a good sized all-terrain Land Rover, complete with towing hook and winch, somewhat younger than the coaches, being post-war at least. "Nice to know you're expecting survivors from this bloody convoy", was Francis dour riposte and turning his attention back to their potential transporters asked when they were booked into the coachbuilders for conversion. On being informed that it would be in one week's time, he squared his shoulders, called a couple of mechanics and commenced the arduous and painstaking process of checking them for mechanical defects, in the full and certain knowledge that without the time to completely strip them down and rebuild them he could not possibly cover everything that might crack up during the long overland journey to Sicily.

At last all was ready and from the car park at the front of the Pegasus factory a hum of excited conversation drifted up to the office where Mike Brookes sat at his desk. Outside, the former coaches waited, one fitted with ramps and a tailgate to carry two precious racers, one fitted out as a mobile workshop to carry as much as could be carried in the way of spares and tools. They and the Land Rover, all newly re sprayed in British racing green with the legend *Team Palm Beach Pegasus Lynx* in gold italics along both sides, sat with engines ticking over, accompanied by the ubiquitous Wyvern. All waited impatiently for Brookes, ready for the off.

Lost in thought, Brookes tapped an index finger on his unusually clear desk until he heard the clip clip of Nicola's heels along the walkway, and looked up as she entered. "Everybody's ready", she began brightly, "we have to be off if we're going to catch the ferry", and then she looked closer. "Are you OK?" she asked. "Just thinking", he replied and shifted in his chair. "I started this as a way to get Pegasus publicity and move the business on but now we seem to be in a position where the whole shooting match could go under unless we get a very good result at the Targa, and that's a damn tough call for any outfit first time out. I never intended that it should be as make-or-break as this". Moving around the desk, Nicola leaned to put an arm around his shoulder. "We'll be fine", she said, "Mark Spall can handle things here; you've put together a fantastic car and you have a team dedicated to its success, now, come on, all we need is a big dose of that pushy Brookes charm and we'll be off. Besides, I don't think I'd fancy you in a bowler hat, and you'd die of boredom working for my dad in The City! Think about it!" Brookes sat up straight in the chair, smiled ruefully at her, took a deep breath and stood. "Let's go", he said, "we've got a bloody race to win!" As he stepped past, she gave him a peck on the cheek followed by a slap on the butt, "that's more like it!" she said.

Followed by Nicola, Brookes strode purposefully along the walkway, down the steps and out into warm Autumn sunshine. "What the hell are you waiting for!?" he bawled, "Christmas!? Let's get this show on the road!" So saying, and followed by a cheer from the assembled throng, he climbed into the driving seat of the heavily laden Land Rover, waited until Nicola seated herself on the passenger side, then led the convoy out of the factory forecourt onto the road that wound its way to the coast and the cross channel ferry.

Big, well established operations such as Cordoba, Ferrari, or Alfa Romeo, regularly engaged in contesting sports car races such as the Targa with their two-car teams, would take anything up to twenty-five or thirty mechanics to   attend every whim and need of the demanding machines – and demanding they most

169

definitely are.   The design of racing cars, particularly sports cars with their gently curving wheel arches and the delicate lines of their bodywork, is overtly sensual, not to say downright sexy, and in temperament the cars are also decidedly feminine – sulky, recalcitrant, and bloody-minded, but when they are on form...

Including Freddie Kendal, Charlie Small, George Stepanek, Brookes, Alan Francis and Harold Cooper, Pegasus boasted ten mechanics to support their two-car team, and that stretched the budget alarmingly enough. With mechanics distributed between all four vehicles, and regular driver changes, the Pegasus convoy made good time into France and headed for the Mt. Cenis pass across the Alps into Italy, the intention being to take the coast road to Naples.   In view of the problems encountered running the race at all, Vincenzo Florio had undertaken to reinstate a service initially offered to attract teams when first his classic race had been run in 1906, and transport the teams by sea from the mainland to Palermo free of charge, an offer that the likes of Pegasus found difficult to refuse. However, in order to take advantage of it they had to be on the quayside at Naples at the very latest mid day Friday 25th October, two days before the race, and the day on which the drivers, Sir Charles Standish, and the Holland & Pendlebury contingent were due to arrive in Sicily by air. As the road ahead of the Land Rover wound inexorably toward the snow tipped Alps, Brookes calculated that they had several days of easy driving in which to get to Naples. He smiled to himself: they should make it with time to spare.

Villages of any size petered out as the Alps were approached, although small hamlets continued into the lower slopes. At midday the convoy made a final halt at one of these hamlets for a last rest stop before pushing on over the Mr.Cenis Pass and into Italy while there was still daylight. Sitting in the small taverna the talk ranged from the journey to their chances in the race, and Alan Francis, who had been driving the second transporter, the travelling workshop, mentioned that the steering had felt a little odd over the last few miles, but opted to get over the Pass first and have a look at it on the Italian side.

Once more the convoy set off and within a few miles the furious honking of a horn and flashing of lights from Alan Francis drew the convoy once more to a halt. Brookes stepped out of the Land Rover and walked quickly back to where the engineer stood by the stricken vehicle. "What's up?" asked the Pegasus boss. "Steering's bollocks'd", replied Francis with feeling, "brackets holding the front axle assembly to the chassis have broken. Bloody thing's going in whichever direction it likes. We have to get it fixed and we can't do it by the roadside, we'll have to turn back for a garage". Brookes thought for a moment. "OK", he said at last, "we'll split up. You take the Land Rover and tow this transporter back to a garage and get it fixed, I'll take the second transporter and the Wyvern and push on over the Pass. Catch us up as soon as you can but we ought to try to get at least a couple of vehicles on one of Florio's ferries. We'll wait for you in Naples for as long as possible. How long d'you think you'll need?" Francis scratched his head. "Well", he mused, "the job itself will take four or five hours, plus we've got to find a garage that can do it...I'd guess we're going to be a good eight to ten hours behind you".

"OK", replied Brookes, "just be as quick as you can. Now, I think Harold Cooper speaks a bit of schoolboy Italian and George Stepanek has some German, so I'll take them with me, along with Charlie Small and a couple of the others. Nicola speaks French and Italian perfectly so she'd better go with you, and you'd better take Freddie Kendal as well. OK?"

"OK Mike, we'll be along as quickly as we can". With the personnel sorted out, Alan Francis and his little band stood by the roadside waving as the remaining two vehicles pulled away towards the mountains. Noticing the deepening, darkening clouds swirling around the Pass, the engineer turned to Nicola. "By the way", he said "did the locals at that last village give you any idea of what weather we're in for?"

"Yes", she responded. "And?" he prompted. "Closing in over the Alps", she said, "low cloud, could well be snow". "Perfect!" said Francis.

The tedious process of backtracking, the Land Rover slowly towing the heavily laden transporter, inclined, as it was, to wander wherever fancy took it, finally ended at dusk, not at the last village passed, which had no garage to speak of, but the one prior to that.

The owner of the establishment, perhaps in his fifties, short of stature, with dark moustache, black unruly hair, and dressed in suitably oily overalls, had just entered the welcome routine of closing up for the day, and perceiving that the vehicles approaching at snail's pace required more than just a fill-up waved his hands and shook his head.

Plainly he looked forward to going home to his pretty, rotund, wife and some of her truly exceptional Gallic home cooking. Despite his voluble protests the vehicles drew to a halt and Alan Francis, accompanied by Nicola, stepped down from the Land Rover while the garage man tapped his watch, flapped his hands, and explained in rapid and uncompromising French that he was tired, closed, going home, and that was that! Come back tomorrow and he would see what could be done, maybe!

Alan Francis got to him first and began to speak, at which point the garage man threw up his hands in exasperation; English! He might have known! This was too much to bear! Turning his back on Francis he waved a hand impatiently – he would hear no more. Come back tomorrow! Francis turned to Nicola, his expression and body language pleading with her to do something. Speaking in fluent French, Nicola began to out line their problem, and slowly the garage proprietor turned. True, he was tired, true, he was hungry, but he was also a Frenchman, and as such always had time for an attractive woman, and Nicola was all of that, and more. Responding to Nicola's entreaties, the man's manner became less strident, but no less negative. He very much regretted, but it was very late, he must get home etc. etc... Glancing over the diminutive Frenchman's shoulder through the still-open double doors leading into the garage, Nicola spied something she thought she recognised, moved past the man and stepped into the garage. A little confused, but still volubly regretting, the garage man turned and followed. Nicola stood in front of a signed, framed, photograph hanging on the garage wall. "Tazio Nuvolari", she said, pointing at the picture. Caught unprepared by the fact that a woman, and an Anglo at that, should recognise a portrait of the great pre-war racing driver, who many said was the greatest, and certainly the bravest, of them all, the Frenchman stopped in mid sentence, mouth comically agape. Taking a gulp of air, the garage man explained reverentially that Nuvolari had passed this way many times before the war on his way from and to races in Italy and all over Europe. On one occasion he stopped at the garage, and had signed the photograph before going on his way to race in the Targa... "The Targa Florio!?" exclaimed Nicola, clapping her hands forcefully enough to make the man jump in surprise. On hearing his confirmation, Nicola took him by the arm and out to the transporter, showed him the name on the side and explained that they too were on their way to race in the Targa Florio, that they had to have the transporter repaired straight away... Suddenly the Frenchman began hopping around in a highly excited manner, clapping his hands together and gabbling so quickly that even Nicola had trouble keeping up with him. It transpired that he had read in the motoring press of the new British team that had managed to bring the legendary Peter Snelgrove out of retirement, and eagerly he looked around, asking if the driver were here. Disappointed at being informed that Snelgrove travelled to Sicily by air, nevertheless the racing fanatic was now hooked, and Nicola deftly reeled him in. If the transporter were not repaired in double-quick time, they might not make it to the race at all, and without all the spares and equipment that it contained, Snelgrove would not be able to drive. Should that be allowed to happen she appealed, hands open, palm outwards in supplication. No! No! No! exclaimed the man excitedly, Snelgrove *must* drive in the Targa, and off he rushed to the telephone to explain to his wife that he had an urgent job to do and might be a little late home.

At 1am the following morning the repaired transporter, followed by the Land Rover, pulled out of the garage and headed once more for the Alpine peaks. Now firm friends with the garage proprietor, Team Pegasus promised to call in whenever they passed his garage, and in addition to handing over a wad of French francs to him for his trouble, Nicola promised to send a signed photograph of Peter Snelgrove to hang beside that other pre-war legend Il Montavano Volante, Tazio Nuvolari, The Flying Mantuan, on the garage wall.

The two vehicle convoy made good progress following the road that wound steadily upwards, sparse lighting to either side disappearing, as predicted, into low cloud over the Pass. With Freddie Kendal driving the transporter and Alan Francis, with Nicola and the remaining members of their little band in the Land Rover, finally, unable to see more than a few yards ahead, they arrived at the Mt.Cenis border post. Having collected all their passports at the garage, Nicola stepped down from the vehicle and over to the border post. The Italian guard inside looked through the documents, while a second strolled around the vehicles and gave them a cursory once-over. It was cold up here and neither felt disposed to stray very far from the stove in the post building. Seating herself back in the passenger seat, Nicola shivered. "They think it will snow tonight", she said. "Right", said Alan Francis, as the pole barring the road swung upwards to allow them through, "let's get off this bloody mountain, it's starting to give me the creeps".

Having passed through the border post into Italy they began the steep descent, and as the mist began to clear a little the occupants of the Land Rover began to feel a little better about their rate of progress. At this point a furious honking on the horn of the transporter behind immediately grabbed their attention and Alan Francis brought the vehicle to a halt. Winding down the window he looked rearwards to the transporter, which had stopped. Muttering obscenities under his breath he got down to the road, "hope to God it isn't that bloody steering again", he said aloud, "we'll never get the bastard fixed up here". Briskly he walked back to the transporter as Freddie Kendal got down from the cab, and the first flakes of snow began to fall. "What's up?" asked Francis. "Back axle", replied Kendal gloomily, "think it's seized". Once more Francis let fly a stream of obscenities, this time aloud. "What the bloody hell else can go wrong with this bastard heap of crap!?" he concluded. As the others drifted back from the Land Rover to see what the problem was, Francis asked Kendal to get back in the cab and see if the transporter would move, so that he could hear for himself what the problem was. Kendal hopped back up into the cab, started the engine, selected first gear and tried to move forward. Immediately a loud grinding issued from the back axle in the area of the differential, and Kendal stopped trying, switched off and got back down from the cab. For what seemed a long moment everyone stood in silence. "What is it?" asked Nicola, and Francis shook his head. "Sounds like the crown wheel or pinion or both have packed up", said Kendal, and Francis nodded in agreement. "What can we do about it?" asked Nicola. "Nothing", responded Kendal, "with the back axle locked

176

we can't go forward or back. We're stuffed well and truly this time". Again a deep silence fell, while Alan Francis began to walk slowly up and down, then stopped, cupped his hands behind his head and looked up into the gently falling snow. "There is one thing we can do", he said. "What!?" asked Kendal. Looking at the younger man, Francis began "we can disconnect the driveshafts and..."

"Are you off your bloody head!?" interrupted Kendal forcefully, "you can't do that! Not up here!"

"Can't do what!?" asked Nicola, "what are you talking about!?" Kendal took a deep breath. "Alan is suggesting that we disconnect the driveshafts and freewheel the transporter down a bloody Alp! Correct!?" he asked looking at Francis. "Correct", confirmed the engineer, "there's no other way we're getting off this frigging mountain with anything like enough time to get to Sicily for the race. When we're down on level ground we can tow this bastard", and here he jerked a thumb at the transporter, "to a garage and get it fixed".

"Wait a minute", offered Nicola, "can't we use the Land Rover to slow the transporter's progress down the mountain?"

"No chance", replied Francis, "loaded the way it is the transporter is much to heavy for the Land Rover to hold from in front or hitched up behind. We'd risk losing both vehicles and everyone in them over a bloody cliff. On the other hand we can't unload the transporter because it's the gear inside that we need, there's no point getting it down the mountain empty". Listening to the wind howl around the otherwise silent mountain for a time, Francis broke into an unexpected smile. "Well" he said, "that seems to be settled so all we need is some silly bugger to volunteer to take the wheel!" Another, and this time not entirely

177

unexpected, silence fell. "I'll do it", Nicola said finally and with serious intent. "The bloody hell you will!" the attendant group chorused in unison, their male egos both bruised and aroused by the very notion. "No", said Alan Francis, "there was never going to be any choice, it's my damn fool idea, I'll do it".

"Hold on", interrupted Kendal, "that's your bloody engine in those race cars, nobody knows them like you so you can't afford to go careering down a mountain risking God know what. I'll take the transporter down".

"Look", said Francis, "it's good of you, but..."

"Come on!" interrupted Kendal, "let's just get on with it!. We can't bloody well stand here all night. There's precious little chance of getting down in one piece as it is, but If this bastard snow settles and starts to freeze there'll be no chance at all!" Francis could see that further argument was pointless, and Kendal was right about one thing – they had no time to waste. So it was that tools were brought hurriedly from the Land Rover, the transporter's driveshafts were disconnected and Freddie Kendal climbed aboard. Alan Francis stood by the door as Nicola moved the Land Rover out of harms way behind the larger vehicle and when all was ready he looked up. "You know of course that the brakes on these things were naff all use when they were new", he said, "so God knows what they're going to be like now, and you've got nothing else to slow you down, no engine, no gears, nothing!?" Kendal looked down and grinned. "You've seen me drive", he said, "I never use brakes anyway! Now stand clear if you please poppa, and I'll see you when this bastard stops rolling. Should be somewhere around Genoa!" So saying he began softly humming *The Runaway Train*, released the handbrake and, freed of all constraint, the transporter began to roll forward.

14.

Some distance ahead, and off the mountain, Mike Brookes and the forward echelon of *Team Pegasus* were also having difficulties, but their problems tended toward the navigational rather than the mechanical. Down here the snow on the mountains turned to slushy rain in the warmer temperature, visibility was minimal and they soon found themselves on a side road and lost. Brookes brought the car to a halt and swore profusely. "Has anybody got *any* idea where the bloody hell we are!?" he asked, more in hope than expectation. Silence ensued, with one exception. From the cramped rear of the car, the plaintive voice of a mechanic asked, "Mike?"

"What!" he answered irritably. "Mike", the voice continued, "where's Charlie and the transporter?" Brookes swore again, wound down the window, stuck his head out and looked rearwards into the driving wet slush, but of Charlie Small and the transporter there was no sign. Brookes brought his head back into the car, closed the window, put the car in gear and began the laborious process of turning the vehicle in the narrow road. "Where are we going?" asked George Stepanek, sitting beside him. "First we're going to find out where the silly bastard in the transporter has got to, then we're going to see if we can find out where the silly bastards in this car are!"

Considerable time was spent driving back and forth looking for their quarry, but to no avail, and Brookes brought the car to a halt once more, this time at a narrow junction. "It's like trying to get out of a bloody maze", he said, "but at least the weather's cleared up a bit". Outside in the pitch black night the driving slushy rain had indeed petered out to a light drizzle. Sitting in the back of the car Harold Cooper wound down his window. "Mike...?" he began. "Yes. What now!?" was the crisp reply. "Mike, those tracks leading off to the right look like they were made by a lorry of some sort..." Brookes opened his door and stepped out of the car to take a look. "Eureka!" he said and turned to Cooper, who still leaned out of the car window. "Well spotted Geronimo", he said, "we had military pattern tyres on both the transporters, very distinctive, I'd recognise those tracks anywhere and there's not much chance that the locals would have them. OK", he continued, climbing back into the car, "let's go find Charlie boy and get out of this damn back of beyond!"

Slowly the Wyvern followed the road and came eventually to a neat village nestling in a shallow valley, and there in the central piazza was the transporter. Brookes parked in front of the lorry and the occupants piled out, grateful to be able to stretch their legs. Brookes checked the larger vehicle for signs of life but Charlie was nowhere to be seen. "Well, let's take a look around and see if we can find him", said Brookes. "Bit early to go banging on doors", responded Harold Cooper, eyeing the first grey streaks of dawn away to the east, "and the locals might not take to a bunch of scruffy Herberts wandering around their village mob-handed". In truth they were an unimpressive sight, not having washed or shaved since the previous morning, so Brookes asked Cooper to accompany him in having a look around while the remainder stayed by the vehicles.

The village was small and clean, and shrubs and pot plants much in evidence gave their final flowering before the onset of winter. The drizzling slush had stopped altogether now and Brookes and Cooper trudged the wet streets looking for signs of life. Eventually they came upon the local bakery, with lights on and the baker inside preparing for the morning rush. Quite apart from not having washed and shaved, the two men approaching had not eaten much either and the smell of freshly baking bread set them salivating. Brookes knocked on the door and pulled it open as the flower bespattered baker looked around. Initially wary at the sight of two dishevelled strangers on his doorstep, he soon became amused at Harold Cooper's attempts to resurrect Italian linguistics that had never been overly good, and had in any event been out of use for many years. Eventually he got the message that they were looking for the young Anglo who drove the lorry into the village late the previous night, and smiling broadly he stepped out of the bakery and pointed across the road to a good sized two storey building with what appeared to be a single storey annexe attached. With a wave and a 'grazi' that even Brookes could manage, the two men stepped across the narrow street and headed for the front door until halted by a call from across the street and a waved hand from the baker indicating that they should go to the annexe.

Stepping through a wrought iron gate beneath a stucco archway, both men entered a narrow passageway and in passing a window in the annexe Brookes stopped and looked through. "Bloody hell", he said, "the bugger's in there sound asleep!" and he tapped urgently on the window. Inside, in the warm comfortable bed in the small neat bedroom, Charlie Small was neither shaken nor stirred and merely raised a lazy hand to scratch an itch on the end of his nose and drift back to sleep. Brookes rapped on the window again and Small opened one eye to gaze at the window. At the sight of the two bewhiskered faces he sat bolt upright in bed. "Bloody hell guv", he exclaimed, "what're you doin' here!"

"Looking for you, you lazy sod!", boiled the Pegasus boss, "now get out of that pit and get your backside out here, quick!" With all the commotion another sleepy head raised itself from the bed beside Charlie, this second arrival, far more pretty that the first and swathed in dark shoulder length curls, belonged to an exceptionally comely young lady. Brookes threw up his hands in exasperation, "I might have known", he said , a hint of admiration leavening his annoyance, "how *does* he do it!" By now Charlie was out of bed and pulling on trousers. Shortly he appeared at a doorway a short distance further along the passageway. "Boss..." he called softly, and Brookes and Cooper stepped through the door and into the warm interior. "Charlie", Brookes began, "words fail me. Where on God's green earth have you been!?"

"Got lost guv", came the abashed reply. "Couldn't see my hand in front of my face in that weather, must've taken a wrong turning and lost you". At that moment the girl, dressed fetchingly in not much more than a short bath robe, emerged from the bedroom. "And just how", asked Brookes, "did you manage to end up here? There must be a hotel of some sort ...?"

"Oh there is guv."

"Well why aren't you in it?"

"No money guv, all my lire's in the Wyvern with you". Cooper chuckled and Brookes shot him a look. "This lady", Charlie continued, "kindly..."

"I *know* what this lady kindly", the Pegasus boss growled, "and anyway I thought you didn't speak Italian?"

"I don't guv".

"Then how...? Oh never mind. Does this lady own the house?"

"Don't think so guv. From what I can make out she's sort of a live-in help. The house is owned by the village doctor and his family".

"And where is the good doctor?" Brookes asked, and Charlie coughed nervously.

"Seems to be away for a few days guv, on holiday".

"Anywhere nice?" asked Brookes with heavy irony. "Sicily, I think guv", replied Charlie innocently, and here the girl intervened. "Yes", she said, her voice heavy with accent, "yes, Sicily, Targa Florio", and here she made engine noises with her lips and moved her hands as if holding a steering wheel, and all the while her spectacular bosom wobbled deliciously under her bath robe. Charlie shrugged sheepishly, "small world" he said, while Cooper burst out laughing and Brookes shook his head in disbelief.

With Charlie and the girl dressed, the group made their way back to the piazza to find that, with the coming of the breakfast hour, a good sized group now gathered around the team vehicles, and much excited chatter filled the air. Brookes and his little band pushed their way through the throng to find George Stepanek in animated conversation with an important-looking, portly, moustachioed, gentleman in his late fifties, who, it transpired, was the village mayor. Not many in the village spoke English and nobody with the vehicles spoke Italian, however thanks to the billeting of German troops in the area for several years during the war, the mayor and

several of the villagers spoke the language, as did Stepanek. Half the village police force, two uniformed carabinieri, attempted to stop Brookes party from making its way through to the centre of the group, but being spied by Stepanek, who called out a greeting, the mayor stepped between the policemen, grabbed Brookes hand in both his own and shook it furiously, repeating "Meester Mike Brookes", several times before Stepanek made formal introductions. Italians the world over are passionately interested in fast cars generally and motor racing in particular; these villagers were no exception and they were just bowled over to have a team bound for the legendary Targa drop in on them, almost literally out of the blue. Now the mayor turned to Stepanek, puffed out his chest importantly, gripped a lapel of his mayoral jacket in each hand and made an announcement in German. Those who understood the language clapped, cheered, and translated for those who did not, and applause and cries of encouragement became general. "What the hell's going on, George?" asked Brookes, perplexed. Stepanek smiled. "They have a small hotel here", he said, "and they invite us all to have a bath and breakfast, on the house".
"Bloody hell, that's damn good of them", responded Brookes, "but time's getting on, we should be on our way..."
"Mike, look at the boys, they'll all be much better off for a good wash and a decent meal, and anyway look around at these faces. They're race fans, we can't disappoint them". Brookes looked around at the eager, expectant faces in the crowd, glanced up at the now cloudless sky, and came to a decision. "Thank the mayor", he said to Stepanek, "and tell him we'll be delighted to accept his kind invitation, and tell him that if he'll promise to have the cops here stand

guard, we'll run one of the racers down from the transporter for the locals to have a look at. OK?" Stepanek relayed the message to his worship, who once again wrung Brookes hand before leading him through the throng to the hotel. Calling over his shoulder, Brookes detailed Charlie Small and two of the mechanics to unload the car and stay with it, taking it in turns to come along to the hotel.

Washed, fed, and feeling much chirpier, Brookes and his half of Team Pegasus sat in the restaurant while the mayor, milking the situation as politicians will, stood to deliver a speech in German, which was, unusually for politicians, mercifully short. Stepanek translated to Brookes his worship's honour and pleasure on behalf of the village at the Team's unexpected and all too short visit and then stopped mid sentence and burst out laughing. The mayor shrugged a little self-consciously and Brookes asked what was so funny. Stepanek recovered his composure and relayed to Brookes the mayor's sincere wishes to Team Pegasus for ' much success in the race and I look forward to seeing your cars come second to a Ferrari!!' Brookes also burst out laughing and stood to shake the mayor's hand. As the speech was translated and word spread the merriment flowed from inside the hotel to the good-sized crowd outside and around the car in the piazza, and much good natured back-slapping camaraderie between villagers and team member's ensued. With the meal completed and the car re-loaded into the transporter, the Team waved a fond farewell to the village as Brookes climbed into the driving seat of the Wyvern. "Right", he said, "let's be on our way or the next thing you know the other transporter will go rolling right past us..."

Rolling the other transporter most certainly was, and at the wheel Freddie Kendal lived a high-speed nightmare. Faster and faster the truck hurtled along the twisting narrow road, while Kendal hauled on the steering wheel to keep the heavily laden vehicle away from the rock face on one side and the beckoning precipice on the other. Virtually standing on the brakes, Kendal could feel the heat from them in the cab while the pungent smell of red hot brake pads caught in his nose and stung his eyes - and as he was fully aware the hotter they got, the less use they became, and the faster the transporter went.

With Alan Francis at the wheel, the Land Rover struggled desperately to keep up with the freewheeling monster ahead, while all marvelled that Kendal did not drop the thing completely off the mountain as the runaway slammed against the rock face, the impact sending the big vehicle slithering across the road, wildly spinning wheel's scrabbling for grip on the very razor's-edge of disaster.

Even in the Land Rover Alan Francis and the ashen-faced occupants could smell the burning brake pads of the runaway transporter, while each impact with the cliff face showered the following vehicle with stones and rocks of all sizes, the most worrying being the smaller, sharper shards that might burst a tyre at any moment and send them all over the precipice.

The wild frenetic ride seemed to Freddie Kendal to have been going on for ever and even through the adrenalin he could feel his arms and shoulders tire as he struggled to keep the heavy brute under some measure of control. Hurtling around a left hand bend he was suddenly aware of a car coming in the opposite direction and did what he could to avoid contact, while being acutely aware that at this speed any sudden movements of the steering wheel on his part would be fatal. Briefly he beheld the terror-stricken faces of the occupants of the car as he flashed past and the transporter surgically removed a wing mirror and a coat of paint from the other vehicle. Once past the car Kendal realised that he was out on flat terrain - he was down the mountain! Now all he had to do was wait for the bloody thing to stop! With the main brakes now completely useless he toyed with the idea of hauling on the handbrake but as that only worked on the rear wheels it would probably spin him around and/or turn him over at this speed, so he settled down to making sure the speeding vehicle did not make serious contact with the scenery at this late stage.

Eventually the big mobile workshop rolled to a halt and the Land Rover pulled up behind. Kendal got down from the cab and the occupants of the smaller vehicle also got out. For what seemed like a long moment there was silence, then Nicola stepped forward to give Kendal a big hug, and, still in silence, one by one the men stepped forward to shake his hand. Leaning on the bonnet of the Land Rover, Alan Francis wiped a tired hand across his forehead. "Bollocks!" he said, aloud and with much feeling, and suddenly the tension of the ride was broken and everyone was laughing and talking and relieved to be in one piece.

15

It was on the quayside at Naples that Team Pegasus was finally reunited. Mike Brookes and his contingent arrived mid day on Thursday, but it was not until Friday morning, with Brookes pacing nervously along the waterfront, that Alan Francis drove the Land Rover into view at snail's pace and pulled to a halt. Coming along behind, Freddie Kendal, once more at the wheel of the transporter, hauled on the handbrake of the slow moving vehicle and it rolled gently into the back of its stationary companion, jarring the teeth of the occupants. Wearily the new arrivals dismounted from their respective vehicles and gathered around Brookes while Alan Francis described their adventures. After the mountain, the Land Rover towed the transporter to a garage where the rear axle was fixed, but the brakes were so badly smashed by the fearful pounding endured that the whole system needed stripping out and replacing, which would have taken too long and used up too much of their dwindling cash reserves. Freddie Kendal volunteered to drive the transporter again and by using a combination of gears, engine, and handbrake, found that he could still bring it to a halt - eventually! Usually the Land Rover followed on behind, but since nobody wanted to watch the lumbering transporter slide with stately grace into the harbour, Alan Francis took the smaller vehicle ahead along the quayside so that Kendal could use it as a buffer if the need arose, which it did.

Having listened with mounting awe to Francis' terrifying tale, Brookes hurriedly got both contingents organised and loaded onto the last of Vincenzo Florio's Palermo ferries. As the ship pulled out of the Bay of

Naples, with Mount Vesuvius brooding sullenly behind the city, Mike Brookes leaned on the taffrail and wondered if he would have started this at all, had he known what it would entail. Probably not, he thought, then smiled to himself. Ignorance is bliss, he mused, and was damn glad he had started it.

Sensing a presence, he turned to find Nicola standing close behind him. Pulling her to him he kissed her. "Hey you", he said, "what's this I hear about you offering to drive that damn transporter down the mountain?"
"We had to get it here", she replied, "anyway Freddie took it on".
"Yes, but I know you, you would have done it if nobody else had, wouldn't you?"
"We had to get it here, we can't race without all the tools and spares". They were quiet for a time, holding each other close, their thoughts their own. Finally Nicola spoke again. "Mike?" she said, and he murmured a response. "Mike", she continued, "you aren't going to drive are you?".
"We have four drivers", he replied, "I'm down as a reserve so that I can practice one of the cars tomorrow. I have to know for myself how they're behaving on the track".
"Yes but in the race, you won't drive in the race will you?". Gently he gave her a squeeze, "we have four drivers", he repeated. Pulling slowly away, she looked at him in that direct way she had. "As team boss you can substitute drivers during the course of a race if you think it necessary", she said. "In Formula One Peter Collins gave up his car during a race and handed it over to Fangio, who was already out of the running, that's why Fangio is World

Champion this year. You're not planning anything like that are you, Mike?"

"No", he replied truthfully, "no, I'm not".

"OK", she said, and he pulled her close again. "Now", he continued, "when we arrive at Palermo I want you to find out what accommodation the organisers have arranged for us and get the team settled while Alan gets us established at our pits..."

"Where will you be?" she asked. "I'm going to take a leaf out of the rally drivers book", he said, "I'm going to drive round the circuit, taking my time and making notes as I go. We have to know what specific problems this race is going to pose for us. OK?"

"OK", she said, putting her arms around his neck and gazing over his shoulder at the receding Italian mainland.

The journey across the Strait of Sicily was a short one and soon Brookes and Francis were supervising the unloading of the Team vehicles. With the transporters and their valuable cargoes safely accounted for, together with all Team personnel, Brookes took a look along the quayside. They were not the only late arrivals for also in evidence was a two-car team of 'D' Type Jaguars, a couple of smartly prepared Porsches and a number of Alfa Romeos of varying types and sizes.

Making slow progress along the quayside, greeting members of each team and studying the cars with interest as they came, a group of five middle-aged gentlemen made their stately progress toward Team Pegasus. Led by a short, slim, balding and moustachioed gentleman of some 74 summers, this was the race organising committee and he was the legendary Vincenzo Florio. Finally the group stopped in front of the British racing green transporters and Florio smiled broadly and introduced himself in halting English. Nicola replied in Italian and soon they were talking like old friends, for it transpired that the old man with the dark, twinkling eyes, remembered their telephone conversations of months previously. As he listened to the conversation, Brookes became aware of somebody standing to his left and he turned so see a man of medium height, heading toward his sixties but evidently in no great hurry to get there, dressed in the best that Italian tailoring and the hand-made shoemaker's art had to offer. "Don Pietro Sevila y Cordoba", the older man said in perfect English, and held out a limp hand, which Brookes shook. "Of Scuderia Cordoba?" asked the Pegasus boss. "Correct", replied the Sicilian, with a slight bow. "I was hoping to see your cars", he continued. "No doubt you will see them on the track", responded Brookes, "we'll be practising tomorrow". At this the Sicilian smiled. "My cars have been practising since yesterday", he said, "there is no substitute for preparation, you know, especially at this circuit. This is your first time at the Targa I believe?"

"Yes, it is".

"Well", the very aristocratic Don Pietro commented idly, "no doubt you will have many other opportunities to make your mark here".

"No doubt", smiled Brookes, "but I intend to make my mark at this one". The Sicilian chuckled indulgently, "you hope to win the Targa at your first attempt? I do not think so, Mister Brookes, why I myself have been trying for many years, but this year I have put together a team comprising the best cars and the best drivers that the world has to offer. I do not propose to be beaten." To the extent of spying on my factory, thought Brookes, but confined his audible response to a non-committal, "we'll see".

"We shall indeed", agreed Don Pietro. Turning to leave, he changed his mind and turned back. "Do you drive here yourself, Mister Brookes?" he asked. "No, not this time".

"A pity", continued the Sicilian with genuine regret, "I saw you race at Le Mans some years ago, you were unlucky that day".

"It happens", the younger man shrugged , "electrics let us down". Don Pietro waved an imperious hand, "a refreshingly philosophical attitude", he opined, "indeed one that you may well feel the need of again, should reality not match your expectations on Sunday". Turning once more to follow his compatriots, the Don retraced his steps back along the quayside. "Who was that?" queried Alan Francis, arriving at Brookes side. "Don Pietro Sevila y Cordoba", replied the Pegasus boss. "Of Scuderia Cordoba?" asked Francis. "The very same", confirmed Brookes.

The entire *Team Palm Beach Pegasus Lynx* personnel were ensconced at the Hotel Posta on via Antonio Gagini in Palermo, perhaps not one of the more ostentatious hotels in the capital, but one that had originally been the residence of the Baroness Dara prior to its re-emergence as a hotel in 1921. Since that time it had acquired a reputation as 'The Artists Hotel', due to its popularity with visiting writers and theatricals, and now played convivial host to contenders in the sporting drama about to be played out a few miles along the coast.

Alan Francis took the transporters with their precious loads, together with the Wyvern and the mechanics, straight out to the circuit to get them settled into their allocated pits, while Brookes took Nicola, Stepanek and Cooper to the hotel. There they found the drivers waiting for them, and a message from Sir Charles Standish saying that he, Takamura, and the Holland & Pendlebury contingent had arrived and were staying amid the Art Nouveau splendour of the Hotel Villa Igiea, built by the Florio family at the end of the 19th century, with its panoramic views, jasmine scented gardens and swimming pool perched above the deep blue Mediterranean.

Nicola swiftly took in hand the business of checking in and getting luggage unloaded from the Land Rover and quickly had Brookes, Cooper, Stepanek and hotel staff depositing suitcases in rooms. Then, with the vehicle quickly emptied, Brookes buttonholed George Stepanek and they climbed aboard and headed for the circuit. It was many years since Stepanek last attended the Sicilian classic, but he was the only experienced head that Brookes had to rely on. Checking in on Alan Francis in the pits, Brookes found the engineer preparing to transport the race cars some 10 kilometres, approximately 6 miles, along the road to the village of Cerda, where scrutineering was in progress. Leaving Francis to it, the Land Rover, with Stepanek at the wheel and Brookes in the passenger seat clutching a wad of plain paper and several pencils, then pulled slowly out of the pits and across the start line for Team Pegasus first 72.5 kilometres in motor racing. Forty-five miles, a single lap of the most gruelling motor race in the world, a race in which teams and cars would have to keep going for lap after lap; for to win the coveted Targa Florio they faced up to eight hours on the very edge of endurance for cars, drivers, and mechanics.

With two days to go to the race, the roads were still open to the public, and normal everyday traffic continued as racing cars hurtled by preparing for the morrow's official practice. Brookes was surprised and amused to watch the Sicilian police hold up farm carts and private cars to allow first one racer and then another to go screaming by. All strictly unofficially, as Stepanek commented, and it could only happen in Sicily.

Stepanek pulled away and the road rose gently to Cerda, with its two-storey stuccoed buildings and balconies from which enthusiastic Sicilians would soon cheer on the racers as they charged by in the street below. Stepanek took the Land Rover past the Birra Messina Bar on their left and out on to the heights above the village, as Brookes took notes. From Cerda the road twisted and turned, dropped down to a river valley and then up to its highest point, the village of Caltavuturo, some 20 kilometres from the startline, and 1000 metres above sea level. Here Brookes called a halt to take stock. It was evident that The Madonie presented a significant problem for cars capable of racing at close to 200 mph. The road was barely wide enough for two cars side by side, never seemed to go straight for more than a few metres at a time, and combined a stomach churning drop on one side with scree-covered slopes rising on the other. From these slopes anything from pebbles to fair sized rocks would roll down to the road below, and each was as dangerous in its way as the other. Rocks might cause punctures and damage suspension components while pebbles acted like marbles, and would be as unpredictable as driving on ice should they be encountered by a car travelling at speed. The Land Rover continued its journey and a few kilometres beyond Caltavuturo, arrived at a fork junction to turn left onto a road built especially for the Targa on the orders of 'Il Duce' himself, Mussolini. At intervals around the circuit gangs of three or four men were employed to clear debris from the track, but their efforts seemed for the most part confined to sweeping everything to the side of the road, where a racing car on the limit could spin its tyres on the 'marbles' and spew them back onto the racing surface.

The road continued its twisting, turning, switchback journey through the village of Scillato and beyond, until it approached Collesano, the stone built cottages of which clung precariously to the mountainside. Here the road snaked along a ledge, and shortly after entering the village executed a sharp left-hand hairpin before twisting its way back out into the mountains, where surrounding peaks would throw back multiple echoes of high performance engines in an ear-splitting cacophony of sound. Brookes stopped for some minutes at the Collesano hairpin, studying the road, taking notes, and chatting with Stepanek.

From Collesano the road dropped down from the mountains to the village of Campofelice, just beyond which it swept left, and there before them was the 6 kilometre long strip of track along the coast. Brookes again called a halt and gave a long, low whistle as he took in the narrow stretch of road, a 'straight' in the true sense of the word. True to form, it was barely wide enough for two cars side by side and was cambered from the centre down to the edges where storm drains lay waiting, ready to rip the wheels off any car that might fall prey to them. Brookes scratched his head with the pencil. The mountains presented significant problems, but this straight was going to be no easier to handle since the most powerful cars, of which the Pegasus was one, would reach speeds approaching 180 mph very quickly along here and a driver would have to maintain that speed while negotiating the uneven surface and struggling to keep the car out of the deep gulleys that formed the drains.

Brookes motioned for Stepanek to continue and the Land Rover resumed its leisurely progress, passed from time to time by other cars, members of the local population going about their daily business in a seemingly incongruous mix with racers screaming by at full 'chat', including, on one occasion, a bright cherry red Cordoba Testa Rossa. 'Nalbandian', said Stepanek, and Brookes nodded, noting the way the car bobbed effortlessly around a tractor-drawn farm cart trundling along the road some way ahead of them, the Argentinean ace having the bucking racer perfectly yet smoothly under his control: car placement, steering and braking free of any of the jerky movements that would have him off the road in milliseconds. "Great driver", murmured Brookes thoughtfully. "One of the very best", agreed Stepenek, followed by "ah, now, here comes the bridge". "Bridge!?" repeated Brookes, his full concentration immediately on the road again, "what bridge?" Stepanek pulled the vehicle to the side of the road and stopped. "Here the River Imera runs from the Madonie into the sea under the bridge". Brookes gaze followed Stepanek's pointing finger and there was the bridge, not by any means a hump back, but it did rise and fall over the waterway, and a driver launching his car over that would need to be very careful indeed about his speed of approach.   One thing, however, gave cause for some relief to the Pegasus boss, neither this road nor indeed any part of this gladiatorial circuit should need to be negotiated after dark, since the race was due to finish in the early evening.

With night now upon them, Brookes looked back and forth along the straight, taking in the high shrubs and bushes lining either side. To comply with the regulations the cars had, in essence, to represent road going vehicles and so had lights, but the almost complete absence of street lighting of any kind would make driving along here after dark at racing speeds a very chancy business indeed. The two men completed the lap and Brookes had them drive around once more, while he continued to make notes. They might not have to race after dark, but shadows cast when viewing the road under headlights showed up bumps, dips, and cambers not normally visible to the naked eye in daylight. Advance knowledge of such critical variations in track surface would be vital to the drivers.

Brookes left instructions that the entire Team, drivers, mechanics, everyone, were to be present at the hotel that evening for a planning meeting, designed to take them over the next two critical days in their fortunes. Nicola arranged for the use of a private function room, as the race attracted much press attention, this year from mainstream journalists as well as the motoring press, thanks to renewed interest in Peter Snelgrove.

The Land Rover pulled in to the hotel parking bay and the two occupants stepped down to walk briskly through a rugby scrum of reporters looking for any titbits of news, which Brookes politely declined to give.   Even outside broadcast cameras for television were in evidence, and pushing through the throng the two men looked around for a familiar face.   Stepanek tapped the Pegasus boss on the shoulder and pointed, and looking in the direction indicated Brookes noticed Nicola waving to him from the far side of the bar.   As he and the engineer reached her she pushed open a door and all three stepped through into a hallway.   Leading the way upstairs they reached the function room, complete with two burly Pegasus mechanics on the door to keep the press away. Briefly stopping to swap good-natured banter with the 'doormen' Brookes and his two companions entered to find everybody there, including Takamura, Sir Charles Standish and one Archibald Drew, marketing director of Holland and Pendlebury.   Drew was a tall, slim, public school type who appeared to have been partaking of the local Marsala to a considerable degree already, but Brookes was pleased to note that, while a number of the Team had drinks in their hands, all seemed steady on their feet.   That was how he intended it should stay, and calling them to attention he explained that, with the race taking place the day after tomorrow, the drinks they held in their hands would be the last alcohol they would have until Sunday evening.   After that they could take Palermo by storm, hopefully with something to celebrate, but until then he expected them to be needle sharp during Saturday practice and on race day, and that meant that they remain sober at night. Rawsnley-Bysh, at his most infuriatingly Oxbridge, piped up that he did not much care for being treated like a schoolboy, and the Pegasus boss snapped back that the if the young man did not like the rules he could go and pack his suitcase right now, and that he, Brookes, would drive the bloody car himself! Nicola shot him a look that could not disguise the concern in her eyes, but she remained silent, as did Rawnsley-Bysh.

Lightening the mood, Brookes turned to Charlie Small and explained, to an accompaniment of much concupiscent banter, that he expected everybody, especially the sexually proclivitous mechanic, to be in their own beds – ALONE! - for the next two nights! Small nodded but looked decidedly crestfallen, for, as he confided quietly to a much amused Freddie Kendal, he was already making promising headway with the slim, attractive hotel receptionist with the deep, dark, eyes, who signed them in when they arrived.

The evening continued with Team personnel switching to soft drinks, although Drew continued to sway to and fro in an invisible breeze and was soon joined by Sir Charles Standish, flushed, and smiling benignly.

Nicola discovered that the hotel employed an English speaking secretary and hurried off to arrange for Brookes' circuit notes to be typed up. Brookes himself called the drivers together for a team talk in a corner of the room and to tell them of their final pairings -Charles Boulet with Rawnsley-Bysh, and Furnley with Peter Snelgrove. The race would last for ten laps, a total of 720 km or 447 miles, meaning a race duration of getting on for eight hours. The previous year, Brookes explained, the fastest lap had been 44 minutes 54 seconds, but in 1955 Moss left the lap record at 43 minutes 7 2/5th seconds, so that was the sort of time they would need to consistently aim at to achieve a good result. Scuderia Cordoba would almost certainly be their principal opposition and he intended to try to discover their driver pairings and pit Snelgrove directly against Nalbandian. He did not say so, but knew perfectly well that the other three drivers were simply not quick enough to challenge the Argentinean, but if, and it was still a big if, Snelgrove retained enough of his old ability he might yet be able rattle the Cordoba team leader. The attitude of Don Pietro during their short conversation on the quay at Palermo indicated to Brookes that the Sicilian did not consider Pegasus to be any threat, and he hoped that the Cordoba drivers, Nalbandian in particular, felt the same way, for if Snelgrove could keep on the Argentinean's pace the unexpected challenge might just force an error, and then...?

Brookes shook the drivers hands and wished them all good luck, and after a decent interval he and Nicola quietly left the throng and made their way to their room. Nicola had already taken the opportunity to bathe and refresh herself after the long journey, and now Brookes did the same, luxuriating in the hot, soapy water. Exiting from the bathroom dressed in a bath robe, with a towel over one shoulder, he found Nicola in front of him bending over her suitcase, her slacks not at all slack over her pert derrière. "Would you mind not doing that?" he asked, a little plaintively. "Doing what?" she replied, looking around. "Bending over", he said. "Bending over?" she repeated, straightening, and then smiled. "Oh, I see", she continued, "you mean the boss is on rations as well?"
"Well, yes, for the next couple of days".
"Couple of days", she replied, holding out a hand to study her fingernails, "what makes you think I'll be interested in a couple of days. I might not be interested for oh a week,

maybe two". Stepping forward he flipped the towel from his shoulder lightly across her bottom. "dames", he said and she turned to put her arms around his neck. Pressing close, she kissed him, and reluctantly he put his hands on her waist and gently pushed her away. "Really", he said, "I have to take the race car out tomorrow and I'm going to need to be as sharp as everyone else".

16

For official practice the circuit opened at first light, clouds scudding across the sky as the first bright streaks of dawn lit the eastern horizon. With roads used for the race now closed to the public, the pits were already an anthill of frenetic activity, and an autumnal nip in the air had drivers and those mechanics not actively involved in preparing the cars blowing into their hands to keep warm.

The Pegasus pit was located at one end of pit lane, close to the circuit, with, to their left the team of Jaguar 'D' types, and beyond them teams of Porches, Alfas, and on down to Scuderia Cordoba at the far end where pit lane rejoined the track. While they would drive alone during the race, Brookes decreed that the drivers would go out and practice in their pairs, one driving, one in the passenger seat reading his notes out loud like the navigator in a rally car. After a few laps they would swap places, and in that way all the drivers should get to know the circuit intimately during the course of the day. As intended, Brookes himself took a car out first, with Stepanek in the navigator role. As the car growled down pit lane and out onto the circuit, Nicola stood in the pit and waved, the worry in her eyes undisguised, for she knew that fast competitive times were called for to be a useful comparison for the drivers, and anyway, Mike did not know any other way to drive a race car.

The first thing that Brookes noticed as he pulled the Seafire racer out onto the racetrack was the vastly differing perspective offered to the driver in a low-slung sports car, compared to the 'crow's-nest' view from the

Land Rover, and he was very glad that they had taken the trouble to detail the circuit the day previously. As the car accelerated away, Stepanek began to read off the notes, shouting both to be heard over the roar of the engine, and penetrate his companion's claret-coloured racing helmet.

Nicola watched the car speed away on the gentle climb up to Cerda, and turned back to the pits. A number of the pit crew busied themselves around the second car while Alan Francis had the remainder get the pit area organised, and Takamura's technicians checked the stock of tyres.

Cars swept along the race track from right to left in front of pit lane, which itself branched off the raceway immediately following the left hand bend that ended the 6 kilometre straight. The start/finish line was situated just beyond the entrance to the pits. Nicola had intended to time the Team Pegasus cars from the pit lane wall, but being unable to see the them approach she found that they came around the corner far to quickly and were gone. Instead she opted to cross the track to the grandstand opposite so that she could pick up the cars as they came down the straight towards her. Stepping through the garage to the Land Rover parked beyond she removed a pair of binoculars, and two clipboards complete with lap charts and twin stopwatches. Back in the pit garage she asked Alan Francis if he had anybody he could spare to come with her and time the Cordoba Ferraris, while she timed the Pegasus cars. Standing within earshot Peter Snelgrove said he would accompany her as he would not be needed to drive until later in the morning.

The two walked along pit lane, several people recognising Snelgrove and calling out greetings, to which he gave a waved reply. Crossing the track was a precarious business but they managed it and positioned themselves a few rows back at the far left of the grandstand. Snelgrove took the binoculars and peered back along the straight; it would be a while before Brookes came into view but one of the Cordoba cars was also out and he spotted the bright cherry red machine as it approached. The car sped around the corner and crossed the start/finish line, Snelgrove noting the number on the lap chart and clicking the first stopwatch on his clipboard into motion. Snelgrove glanced at Nicola and could see the tension in her eyes. "He'll be alright", he said, and she smiled an uncertain smile. "I wish he didn't have to drive at all", she replied. "Well", responded Snelgrove, "Mike's being thorough. It's all very well us telling him what the track is like and how the cars are handling, but if he has a feel for both himself it will give him a much better idea of how to tweak the racers to get the best out of them".
"Yes, of course I know that, but, well, you know..."
Snelgrove nodded and Nicola changed the subject, "but how about you?" she enquired, "how are you feeling?"

"About tomorrow?", he said, and paused. "A little nervous", he continued, peering down the long straight, "but that's nothing new, I always felt a certain amount of tension before a big race. It's not necessarily a bad thing you know, it can sharpen your performance, it's only if you get nerves in a really bad way that it destroys your concentration". Nicola smiled and suddenly Snelgrove gasped and leant forward. "Are you alright?" she asked quickly, and slowly he straightened. "Yes", he said, "a touch of indigestion, I went into Palermo last night and I'm not used to this rich Italian food". Rubbing a hand across his lower chest, he glanced at her, noticed her quizzical look, and smiled. "Don't worry", he said, "I rarely drink and last night wasn't one of the occasions when I did. I've been pestered by journalists since I got here so I thought I'd see if they might be of some use to us".

"How?"

"Well, while they pumped me about my comeback, I pumped them about Nalbandian".

"Get anything useful?" she asked, taking the binoculars..

"Maybe", he mused, "they all think he's one of the best there is, that's for sure. They think he'll win, but the British guys hope that at least we'll give him a run for his money". He paused for a moment. "One or two of them", he continued slowly, "said they thought there might be, not weaknesses exactly, but a grey area or two in his driving armoury".

"Anything you can make use of?"

"I'm not sure. He's never done much wet weather driving and when he does he tends to be a bit conservative. Not that he's slow, it's just that wet weather takes the edge off that famous brio of his. What's the forecast for tomorrow?"

"We might well get rain", she responded, "but it's not expected until late afternoon. The race may well be over by the time it gets here. What's the other thing?"

"Well, that will be even less use", Snelgrove said, "being principally a Grand Prix driver, he's apparently never done any night racing, so that's an unknown factor, but in any event the race should be over before dark".

"Well, you'd better tell Mike and the others anyway".

"Yes of course. I think I may have the Cordoba driver line-up as well. I'll tell Mike when I see him".

"Yes good, and speaking of Mike", she said, peering along the straight through the binoculars, "here he comes". Shortly afterwards the dark green race car sped through the corner with a screech of tyres, and Nicola clicked the first stopwatch to commence timing his first flying lap. "Not hanging about, is he?" said Snelgrove, while Nicola pursed her lips and nodded apprehensively.

Brookes did four laps including his out lap, and from the far end of pit lane each was timed by Cordoba team manager Salvatore Castellotti. Leaning over his shoulder Don Pietro took the lap chart when he saw the Pegasus pull into pit lane. Glancing down he read the times, "an out lap of over fifty minutes", he said, "first flying lap forty eight minutes ten seconds, second flying lap forty six minutes, third flying lap a little slower".

"I expect that would be the new radial tyres Pegasus are using", offered Castellotti. "The rumour is that they are good for three laps, no more". Don Pietro stared at the lap chart. "Still..." he said, deep in thought, "their car is good, and Brookes..."

"...Is not as fast as Nalbandian", interrupted Castellotti, sensing an onset of the aristocrat's usual pre-race nerves, "he does not have the pace of the Argentinean..."

"...it is perhaps true that he does not have the raw driving skill of Nalbandian", responded Don Pietro, "but remember I have seen him drive before, he is brave, brave as a Moss, possibly even a Nuvolari. A driver needs to be brave on this circuit". Heaving a sigh he handed the lap chart back to his team manager. "I think", he said, "that the biggest mistake that Mister Brookes has made this weekend is not to drive the car himself. Now, we have the driver pairings arranged for tomorrow, yes?"

"The word is", said Peter Snelgrove, munching a breakfast sandwich in the Pegasus pit, "that Nalbandian will partner Falletti, and the Argentinean will do the first and last stints..."
"...That's to be expected", said Brookes, "he's their quickest, stands to reason they'd use him to start and finish".
"In the second car", Snelgrove continued, "von Schmidt will partner Fondi, another Italian, that way if either of his cars wins, Don Pietro will have at least one Italian driver in it".
"OK Peter, that's it then", said Brookes, "tomorrow you drive against Nalbandian. You'll do the first and last stints for us".
"That's fine by me, Mike". Brookes put a hand on the driver's shoulder, "rattle his cage, Peter", he said, "if you don't let him settle into a rhythm we might just have the ghost of a chance. Now, finish your bloody breakfast and get in the car, we've got a practice session to get on with!"

Snelgrove finished the sandwich and picked up his racing helmet, a new one, silver like the original, but with a visor and without the flags. Resplendent in his racing green overalls, as were the rest of the team, the driver pulled gloves out of the upturned helmet, which he then placed under his arm as he stepped out into the bright morning sun of pit lane. Pulling on the gloves he glanced across to the wall between pit lane and the racetrack and noticed a round-faced dark haired youth in his early teens looking at him intently. Taking the helmet from under his arm and dropping it to his side, Snelgrove glanced up and down pit lane and trotted across to where the boy stood. "Hello", he said, "I'm Peter Snelgrove". The boy smiled nervously, "I know", he replied, the voice thick with accent. "What's your name?" asked the driver. "Nino", the boy replied, "Nino Vaccarella".

"You like cars, Nino?"

"Oh yes, too much I like racing cars".

"Are you Sicilian?"

"Yes Signor Snelgrove, I am Sicilian".

"And what are your favourite cars?"

"Oh Ferrari", the boy enthused, "one day I will drive for Ferrari".

"Well", said Snelgrove, smiling, "the only Ferraris here are down at the other end of pit lane, in the Cordoba pit".

"I know", replied Nino, "I was there and I have the autographs of Signor Nalbandian and the other drivers, but the team they don't like me to stay around the cars".

"Is that so..."

"Signor Snelgrove...?"

"Peter, the name's Peter". Carefully Nino reached into a jacket pocket and withdrew a pen and a small brown leather covered book. "May I have your autograph also?" he asked. "I'll do better than that", said Snelgrove, taking book and pen, "how would you like to come across to our pit for a while – we don't run Ferraris I'm afraid, but you might find it interesting". The young Sicilian's face broke into a broad grin as the driver signed a page of the book and handed it back to him. Taking the youngster's shoulder, Snelgrove guided him across pit lane to the garage, and spying Brookes, hailed him. "This is Nino Vaccarella", he told the Pegasus boss, "a future race driver and Ferrari fan, but they won't let him stay around the Cordoba garage. OK if he stays here for a while?"

"Fine", said Brookes, "but Nino, don't get in the way, OK?" So saying he stuck out a hand, which, smiling broadly, the young Sicilian shook. "OK Signor Brookes", he said, "OK!"

The team quickly warmed to the keen enthusiasm of the youngster as he watched the comings and goings of the cars, and the busy workload of the mechanics. Finally, having had lunch along with everyone else in the garage, he bid them a cheerful goodbye and went on his way clutching numerous souvenirs of his stay, his autograph book nearly full.

For the Targa circuit the Pegasus cars were fitted with four close ratios for the mountain section, plus a high 'overdrive' fifth for the long straight. Following his first stint, and discussions with Stepanek, Snelgrove suggested some ratio changes, including a higher fifth gear that would give them more pace down the straight. The alterations were made and led to an immediate improvement in lap times. This year, as usual at the Targa, lap times were not to count toward grid places as in other races. Cars were scheduled to start one at a time at thirty second intervals, beginning with the slowest class, not much more than road machines, and proceeding to the thoroughbreds, the Ferraris, Porsches, Alfas, Jaguars, and Pegasus. This posed an additional hazard for drivers of the faster machines, since, by the time they got away, the road ahead, especially the narrow mountain sections, would be crowded with much slower cars. Nevertheless all the teams put maximum effort into obtaining good times, and as expected Nalbandian came out quickest, despite competing in only his first Targa, with a time of forty five minutes fifty two seconds. Second was Fondi, something of a Targa specialist, this being his third outing in the race, posting forty six minutes forty eight seconds. Much to the delight of Mike Brookes and Pegasus, Snelgrove put in three very quick laps, his fastest being forty seven minutes five seconds for third fastest. The remaining Pegasus drivers all put in reasonable times, Rawnsley-Bysh, despite being too ragged and 'on the edge' for Brookes liking, quickest at forty nine minutes, for sixth place behind a Jaguar and an Alfa.

As Team Pegasus packed up their pit for the day, the mood was buoyant, with many a happy tune whistled, although one or two members of the crew, including Brookes, glanced skyward at gathering steel-grey cloud overhead and wondered what that might portend for the following day.

As darkness fell the heavens opened and that night in the hotel room, lying next to Nicola's quietly sleeping form, Mike Brookes lay awake listening to rain beat furiously against the window pane as lightening flashed across the night sky, and thunder rolled deep and ominous across the mountains of the Madonie. Finally, in the early hours, the storm eased and Brookes drifted gratefully off to sleep.

With the race due to start at 10am, Brookes was awake, washed and dressed as the imminent arrival of the sun spread a deep pink glow across the eastern horizon, and clouds hung in silhouette dark in the skies above. Calling through to Nicola in the bathroom that he would wait for her downstairs, he left the room and trotted down to find most of the crew already up and about, and two messages waiting for him at reception. The first was from Mark Spall asking him to call urgently, and the second from the race organisers explaining that the storm the previous night had caused a landslip in the Madonie mountains and the track was blocked. Road crews were already out clearing the obstruction, but the start of the race had been put back to 11am. The message concluded by requesting him to wait at the hotel for further news. Showing the message to Alan Francis, it was decided between them that the engineer would take the crew out to the circuit to make final race preparations while Brookes, aided by Stepanek and Snelgrove as the two most experienced members of the team, would await developments at the hotel. The three were soon joined by Nicola and the group decided to kill a little time by taking the opportunity to enjoy a light breakfast in the restaurant, the thoughts of all on the implications of the delay, and impatient for news.

Following breakfast the group adjourned to the armchairs of the coffee room to chew over the prospects and enjoy numerous cups of superb Italian coffee, while Nicola periodically telephoned the race organisers for news, of which that there was none, save that Vincenzo Florio himself was looking into the matter but was not presently at the office.

Brookes placed a call to Mark Spall which came through unusually quickly. Spall explained with barely concealed worry in his voice that La Grange, the bank manager, was racking the pressure up again, worrying and fretting and talking about needing more security. It was, explained the finance director, vital that the team secure the best possible result at the race otherwise there might not be a Pegasus to come back to. Brookes replaced the telephone receiver and decided to keep this particular piece of news to himself.

With the time approaching 10am, the group in the coffee room was joined piecemeal by Takamura, Archibald Drew, and lastly Sir Charles Standish, who arrived flushed and breathless and bringing news of a sort. "The word is", Standish said, "that the start will now have to be delayed beyond eleven. Florio has been out taking soundings from all the team owners and is apparently on his way here now to see you".

With only a second or two to consider the implications, Brookes noticed Vincenzo Florio enter, flanked by Don Pietro Sevila y Cordoba and members of the race organising committee. "Nicola", said Brookes, standing to greet the new arrivals, "let's see what they've got to say". With Nicola standing beside him, Brookes shook hands warmly with Florio, who got straight to the point. "The race start", Nicola interpreted, "will have to be delayed until twelve noon, which means that, if kept to ten laps, will not finish until after dark. We have visited all the team owners for their views on the possibility of reducing the race duration to eight laps and they are evenly split between those who wish to foreshorten the race and those who wish to keep it to the original length. I hope you will not be offended, but as the newest entrant we came to you last". Brookes smiled indulgently as Florio continued, "we came to you last in the hopes that the decision would already have been reached, but it seems that instead we

213

have to impose upon you the casting vote. Would you like to discuss the matter with your companions?" Florio asked in conclusion. Brookes nodded and was about to turn to his group when Don Pietro spoke up. "Mister Brookes", he said in that faintly condescending way that he affected, "there is no reason to prolong the race until after dark. You are a new entrant and it can be of no benefit to you to run the extra two laps, it will only cause you problems. Please take my advice", he continued, "and accept the shortened race. It is the sensible thing to do". Brookes pursed his lips thoughtfully and turned to the assembled group. "Well", he said, "let's see; Charles, what do you think?"

"You're running the team", replied Standish, "it's your decision, but I think Don Pietro's right. The longer duration will be of no benefit to us". Glancing at Takamura he asked for the Japanese' opinion. "From the point of view of tyre wear", the Japanese responded, "the shorter duration must benefit us". Archibald Drew also came down on the side of the shorter race, and Brookes turned to Stepanek. "Peter has to drive that last stint", said the Polish engineer, "I will accept whatever he says", and Brookes turned to Peter Snelgrove. The driver looked intently at his shoes for a second or two, then looked up and straight into Brookes eyes, "go long" he said simply, and both men smiled briefly. Finally Brookes turned back to Nicola, who recognised the look on his face and glanced to the ceiling and back, "go long?" she asked, and he nodded. Don Pietro raised his hands heavenwards in frustration and began to harangue Florio in staccato Italian, until the race organiser raised his hand for the nobleman to cease while Nicola relayed Brookes decision. Upon hearing the result of their deliberations the Sicilian smiled and held out his hand, which Brookes shook warmly. "thank you", Florio said in heavily accented English, "the race will be ten laps as originally planned, seven hundred and twenty kilometres", he paused, "I believe that is", he said slowly, "four hundred and forty-seven of your British miles".

17

Rain clouds continued to scud across the autumn sky, but by twelve noon all thirty-four competitors were assembled line-astern and the first, the Fiat 600 of Fabio Colonna, was waved off the start-finish line. Thirty seconds later the second car, the Lancia Appia of Piero Taruffi, sped away, and so, at thirty second intervals, did succeeding cars until the moment approached that the vast crowd dispersed through the grandstands and around the circuit were waiting for, the roar of the big three-litre sports cars, one of which would undoubtedly be declared winner in around eight hours time. First of the big beasts away was Nalbandian in the Ferrari, followed by Cordoba team mate Von Schmidt. Third up to the start line growled the Pegasus of Peter Snelgrove. As the thirty seconds were counted off, Snelgrove gave Brookes, standing in the crowd, the thumbs-up, flipped down the visor on his helmet and as the chequered flag came down, gunned the engine and roared off in pursuit of the Ferraris. Brookes waited long enough to see Rawnsley-Bysh safely away a few cars later, and returned to the pits. "Well", he said, "they're both away. Everything ready here?" Alan Francis nodded, his only outward sign of the tension within being the more or less constant wiping of his hands on a piece of rag.

By the time the big sports cars reached Cerda they were already in amongst the slower cars and Snelgrove tweaked the powerful Pegasus this way and that, deftly passing first one then another as he sped through the narrow streets of the village in pursuit of the Ferraris. Exiting the village a straight section of road led up a slight incline and he glanced in the rear view mirror. Behind him came the first of the two Jaguars, followed by a Porsche. He couldn't see Rawnsley-Bysh in the sister car. With full concentration back on the road ahead his attention focused on his first objective, the Ferrari of Von Schmidt as it disappeared around a corner, the German ace impatiently seeking his chance to pass a gaggle of slower cars.

The race organisers had arranged for a number of marshal's posts around the circuit, all connected to race control by telephone, their function, in the absence of stranded cars to attend to, being to telephone race reports back to race control to enable continuous commentary over the public address system. In the Pegasus pit it was one of Nicola's jobs – another was to keep the lap chart - to listen to the commentary for any news of the team cars. With one ear on the commentary, and the best part of three-quarters of an hour to dispose of before the cars flashed by in front of the pits and across the start-finish line, Nicola strolled across pit lane and sat on the wall that separated the pits from the racetrack. Opposite stood the now packed main grandstand, where moneyed Sicilians and race cognoscenti paid to see and (just as importantly) be seen, despite the fact that they could observe the event for free anywhere else around the lap distance. It was evident from her observations of the grandstand occupants that for the Sicilian upper-strata the Targa Florio occupied a place somewhat similar to that of Ascot in England. The ladies sported much extravagant finery, with less ornate, but nevertheless smartly turned out gentlemen in attendance. Lunch appeared for the most part to combine the sipping of champagne with the nibbling of delicacies created by chefs from all the bounty that the island and the surrounding seas could offer. Nicola smiled. It was all very genteel and really quite appealing.

In response to the Mille Miglia accident a high reinforced fence had been erected around the outside of the corner after the straight and stretching along the front of the main grandstand, but for the remainder of the circuit there was not so much as a chicken-wire fence to separate spectators from the cars. Consequently, excited and enthusiastic race-goers, getting on towards a quarter of a million of them, could be something of a problem. Snelgrove managed to get up close behind Von Schmidt in the traffic and was lining up to make a pass along 'Mussolini's road', the fast downhill section beyond Caltavuturo. Right on the Ferrari's tailpipes as the cars twisted through one bend after another, the Pegasus driver bided his time until Von Schmidt made a small mistake and drifted a little too wide into a sharp left hand bend. In an instant Snelgrove was up on the inside of the Ferrari, and side by side they scorched through the corner. With the inside track, the Briton was sure he was through, but as they exited the corner, Snelgrove's heart seemed to leap in his chest and the breath caught in his throat as he saw a Sicilian run across the track from right to left, his arms full of bottles of the local beer. Von Schmidt jinked right and past the kamikaze spectator but Snelgrove was forced to brake hard to avoid him. As the spectator scrambled up a grass bank, more intent on not dropping the bottles than his narrow escape, Snelgrove gunned the motor and set off once more after the German, but now with the quicker of the two Jaguars to contend with, agitating to get past before the Pegasus was back up to racing speed.

By the wall along pit lane Nicola was suddenly all attention as the commentator, who's excitable delivery gave the clear impression that his trousers must be alight, gabbled about an incident out on the circuit. Rushing back to the pit, Nicola relayed the news to Brookes, Alan Francis, and everyone else in earshot. Peter was up with Von Schmidt and put a move on him that did not come off – the commentator did not say why – and now Peter was having to fight off the Jaguar. Nicola relayed more news as it came in until Brookes glanced at his watch and all three, followed by most of the pit crew, crowded along the wall to watch the end of the first lap. Within minutes Nalbandian roared past, and Nicola entered his time on the chart. Brookes studied his watch until Von Schmidt, Snelgrove, and the Jaguar flashed by nose to tail. "Nalbandian's pulling out a lead", murmured the Pegasus boss, "he's one minute twenty-eight seconds ahead. Peter has to get by that second Ferrari and get after him, he can't be allowed to settle into a rhythm or we'll never catch him".

Almost as one the second, third, and fourth placed cars blasted up the incline towards Cerda and entered the narrow road through the village. At the far end the driver of a Renault Dauphine seemed to be out not so much for a race as a Sunday afternoon drive. Suddenly awake to his perilous situation, he discovered his rear view mirror to be full of three racers, engrossed in a duel of their own, closing on him with frightening rapidity. With barely enough room to get by, Von Schmidt had to make a split second decision and moved right. Unfortunately for him, in its efforts to get out of the way, so did the Dauphine, badly baulking the Ferrari. Like lightening held over from the previous night's storm, Snelgrove, closely followed by the Jaguar, was through. Von Schmidt slammed on the brakes in a slithering, sliding, cloud of tyre smoke, and furious with the driver of the diminutive French car, waved his fist angrily as he recovered and sped by, determined to regain the lost places.

With the Pegasus handling perfectly and the radial tyres giving phenomenal grip, Peter Snelgrove noted with relish that the track ahead was, for the moment, free of back markers and began to pile on the pressure, pulling inexorably away from the Jaguar, (which now also had Von Schmidt in full red-mist mode to contend with). For Snelgrove the problem was, for the moment, simplified, and he meant to take maximum advantage of it. Somewhere up ahead was the hard-charging Nalbandian, and the Briton meant to catch him.

In the pits, Mike Brookes and the Pegasus crew knew something was up even before Nicola relayed the news. The animated chatter up and down pit lane and the evident excitement in the grandstand opposite told their story, as Nicola bustled in to fill in the details. Snelgrove was up to second, and from provisional timings between marshal's posts seemed to be catching the Argentinean. Like all Italians, Sicilians love to see a Ferrari win, but almost as much they like to see a real motor race, and that was precisely what they sensed was in progress out there on the track as the determined old campaigner served notice that the new boy on the block was not going to get things all his own way.

As Nicola explained what was going on, the news exploded across the Pegasus pit. With the racer in him fully restored, Sir Charles Standish clenched his fists and loudly urged Snelgrove on. Archibald Drew hopped from one foot to another, wiped his lips and nervously scratched his head, while Takamura smiled quietly to himself and had his engineers check the replacement tyres one more time. Brookes glanced at Alan Francis. They said nothing but the look from both men said it all – can we *really* do this? Brookes snapped himself out of the euphoria and clapped his hands loudly, "OK", he said, "this is good news, but we've still got hours of racing ahead, let's get down to business. Make sure everything is checked and rechecked, I don't want any cock-ups during the pit stops".

Sprinting across pit lane to the wall, Brookes was in time to see the lead Ferrari scream out of the corner and past the pits. Clicking his stopwatch he waited, the nervous tension in him building for one minute twelve seconds, when the dark green Pegasus also hurtled by. He turned to find Nicola and Charlie Small standing by him, Nicola with the lap chart, Small pulling in a pit board which said simply, 'Peter. Catching Nalb.' "Peter made up sixteen seconds on that lap", Brookes said. Nicola nodded, and Small whistled softly. "The Cordoba pit boards will have told Nalbandian that Peter is after him", the Pegasus boss continued, "so let's see how he handles that piece of bad news".

The Argentinean handled the situation like the racer he was and for a time stabilised the gap, but Peter Snelgrove was driving the race of his life, and knowing that

Nalbandian would now be aware that he had a race on his hands, pushed all the harder.

Barely able to contain her excitement Nicola relayed the news to the pit that, after a short hiatus, Peter was again catching the Ferrari. With Brookes pacing nervously up and down, some forty minutes into the lap a much subdued Nicola passed on the unwelcome fact that Peter seemed to be dropping back, and the gap was widening. Brookes cursed out loud and clapped a hand to his forehead. From the rear of the pit garage Takamura stepped forward, "it may be the tyres", he said in his halting English. "We designed them to last for three laps, but Peter had been pushing very hard, and the circuit is very tough, perhaps the wear rate is more than anticipated". Brookes grimaced, "OK", he replied thoughtfully, "we'll soon see, he's due in shortly and we can check the tyres then". Turning on his heel he bellowed for Piers Furnley, only to find the driver standing next to him, pulling on gloves. "Now, Piers", the Pegasus boss continued, "you know the situation, we've been catching the Ferrari, but we have a problem that may or may not be tyres. Wait there until Peter gets out of the car and we'll see what he says. OK?" Looking tense but focused the driver nodded, donned racing helmet and buckled the chinstrap.

Hearing the lead Ferrari growl past in pit lane, Brookes sprinted to the front of the garage to watch it pull into the Cordoba pit. "Everything ready?", he barked, turning to Alan Francis. The engineer nodded, and in seemingly no time, Snelgrove pulled up in the dark green sports car and jumped out to appreciative applause from those mechanics not actively descending on the racer. Quickly a mechanic rolled a trolley jack under the front of the car, while at each front wheel a mechanic tapped loose the central wheel nut. The first mechanic put his weight on the jack and the front of the car lifted off the ground. In an instant the front wheels were changed and the mechanics sprinted to the rear to repeat the process. Snelgrove pulled off the silver helmet and Brookes noted with a start how pale and drenched in perspiration the driver was, but there was a fire in his eyes that the Pegasus boss had not seen there before. Glancing down at the old front wheels with their badly worn tyres, Snelgrove nodded, "thought so", he said. Turning to Furnley, he spoke quickly. "Car's a beaut!" he said, "handles like a dream, so did the tyres for two laps or so, but halfway around the third lap they went off quickly. While the tyre's work we can catch the Ferrari, so get after it early on!"

With the rear wheels changed in double quick time, Charlie Small finished emptying a large can of fuel into the car's tank and glanced along pit lane. "Ferrari's away!" he yelled and Brookes slapped Furnley on the back. "Go!" he snapped, and the driver dashed to the car and leapt in. Immediately, Freddie Kendall stepped forward, snapped closed the racing harness, Furnley gunned the engine and roared off in pursuit of the Cordoba machine.

Brookes turned back to see Peter Snelgrove slumped at the back of the garage, head in hands. "Peter", he said, "that was one of the most amazing bloody drives I've ever seen!" Snelgrove looked up and smiled. "What will we do about tyre wear?" he asked. Once more Brookes looked around and found Takamura and his tyre engineers closely

223

inspecting the discarded tyres. "Well?" he asked, and Takamura stood and walked over, his expression grim. "Tyre wear is more than anticipated", he said. "The tread is worn flat in places and breaking up in others. In that condition they could well be dangerous at racing speeds". Brookes bit his lip, the unspoken thought on each man's mind the final stint of the ten lap race. Four laps. "Peter", Brookes said after a moment's thought, "you were substantially quicker than the Ferrari for two laps, weren't you?" Snelgrove nodded. "Well", continued the Pegasus boss, "you'll have to come in for an extra tyre change and we'll just have to hope that we don't lose too much time. We'll split your final drive into two sections of two laps each". Snelgrove smiled. "Perhaps", he said, "we should have voted for the eight lap race after all". Brookes gave a wry smile. "Too late for that now", he said, "Shoji, do we have enough tyres for an extra stop?" The Japanese nodded, "yes", he said, "but only for one car. What about the second car?"

"We'll explain the tyre problem and they'll just have to take it easy. They might still manage a decent placing if other cars drop out ahead of them". Brookes wiped a hand across his forehead, hoping he had thought of everything. Glancing down at Snelgrove he told the tired driver to get something to eat and drink then take a rest in the Land Rover. With all the spares from that vehicle now in the garage he could lower the front seats and try to get some sleep. Snelgrove nodded, stood, and pulled off his driving gloves. Brookes noticed the bandaged right hand and raised an eyebrow. "Helps stop blistering", said the driver, "with all the gear changing here that can be a nightmare". Brookes nodded, "good idea", he said. "Now, where's Rawnsley-Bysh?"

Adrian Rawnsley-Bysh winced in pain as he grabbed the gear lever to change gear yet again. With 832 bends and corners on every lap, and gear changes required for most of them, the palm of his right hand felt red raw under the glove. Still fuming over the stupid mistake on the first lap and now on his third and final lap for this stint he hurled the car along the approach to Campofelice as the Jaguar in front exited the little village and turned onto the 6km straight before the pits.

But his mind was still half on the first lap, that bloody first lap, on the approach to Cerda just after the start he snatched fourth gear instead of third, the car faltered and the second of the two Jaguars, a Porsche and an Alfa Romeo went past him as if he were tied to a post. Recovering quickly he set off after the pack, and had to admit that the car felt good. Getting his foot down he took back a place from the Alfa that same lap, and another from the Porsche on the subsequent tour. Now, approaching the end of the third lap, just the Jaguar remained, and as Rawnsley-Bysh exited picturesque Campofelice and turned onto the arrow-straight 6km section, he floored the accelerator and felt the car surge forward. Up ahead the Jaguar approached the bridge and seemed much closer. Rawnsley-Bysh pressed on, certain that he could pass the car in front before the end of the lap; as he reached the bridge he lifted off the accelerator and dabbed the brake. The bridge did not rise much above road level, but even so the car felt very light until it regained the road on the other side. The Jaguar was very close now, and pulled to the outside of the road. Rawnsley-Bysh saw his chance and accelerated hard to pass down the inside, but the Jaguar now moved to the left and in that horrifying fraction of a second Rawnsley-Bysh realised both that the Jaguar must be moving over to pull into pit lane, and that he was carrying far too much speed to get into the pits himself. Slamming his foot hard on the brake pedal he made an attempt to negotiate the corner, and with new tyres he might just have made it; but these were badly worn, and in milliseconds Rawnsley-Bysh made the transformation from driver to passenger as the car careered across the road and hit the fencing on the outside of the sharp left-hander. A front tyre burst with the impact and the car lifted and cart wheeled along the fencing in front of the grandstand, finally coming to rest on its side, wheels facing the grandstand and slowly spinning to a halt. Spectators chattered and gesticulated animatedly, some stood, some pointed at the wreckage.

Rawnsley-Bysh had been travelling along the straight at close to 180mph and in seconds endured the crash and came to a juddering halt, half hanging out of the racing harness. Stunned and confused by the impact he hung there motionless for what seemed like an age. Then he smelt the petrol.

Knuckles white as he gripped the pit wall, Brookes watched the car screech and tear its way along the fence opposite and come to rest on its side. Rawnsley-Bysh did not move, just hung there half out of the harness. Brookes turned and the first person he saw was Charlie Small. "Get a fire extinguisher" he yelled, "and follow me!" As he spoke he vaulted the pit wall, glanced quickly toward the corner for oncoming cars, then dashed across to the wreck. Reaching the car he tried to release the harness but the weight of the driver hanging in the straps made it impossible. Hearing the hiss of the fire extinguisher behind him, he turned. "God Almighty!" exclaimed Charlie Small as he sprayed foam over the wreck, "there's petrol everywhere, this bastard lot's going up any minute!"

"Charlie!" shouted Brookes, "come here, quick, release the harness when I take his weight!" Charlie ran to the cockpit and Brookes took the driver's weight on his shoulders as the mechanic hit the harness quick release clasp. Released from the belts Rawnsley-Bysh fell and Brookes stumbled under the burden, the two hitting the ground heavily, the driver crying out in pain. "Come on guv!" yelled Charlie, "grab his arms, the frigging thing's alight!" Getting to his knees, Brookes grabbed Rawnsley-Bysh under one arm as Charlie Small grabbed the other. Again the driver cried out in pain as he was dragged away. Charlie felt the hairs on the back of his neck stand on end as he heard the terrifying 'whoosh' of petrol catching fire behind him. Having made the few steps to safety the two men half lowered half dropped their burden and fell, winded and scared, but out of reach of the fire. Raising himself up on his elbows Mike Brookes blinked and watched the car burn, then glanced down at the driver. Rawnsley-Bysh tried to sit up, but groaned and fell back. "Any chance of a drink, boss?" he asked. Also sitting up, Charlie Small agreed. "Oh blimey yes", he said with feeling, "a cool pint would go down a treat just now". Seeing the two men stumble away from the wrecked car dragging a third, and seeing Rawnsley-Bysh move, applause and shouts of encouragement rippled around the grandstand and spread to the pits across the road. Within minutes race marshals and first aid staff arrived to carry out a quick examination of the driver before loading him onto a stretcher to move him to safety away from the track

227

side.　"Charlie", gasped Brookes, "I've got to get back to the pits, stay with them until they've given him a thorough once over.　See how he is, OK?"

"OK guv", replied the mechanic, getting to his feet and following the medics.

18.

With the first driver changes of the race completed Nalbandian had relinquished the lead car to Faletti, Furnley now drove the second placed Pagasus, and, having passed the Jaguar, Von Schmidt handed his Ferrari to Fondi in third. Initially Faletti opened the gap a little but Furnley quickly settled into a rhythm, had the gap pegged back to one minute thirty seconds and held it there. His problem was that behind him Fondi used all his knowledge of the Targa to pile on the pressure, steadily closing on the second placed Pegasus.

Things settled down again for a time, and Charlie Small returned to the pits with news of Rawnsley-Bysh. The harness and the inherent strength of the spaceframe design restricted fractures to a broken ankle, but that same rigid strength, combined with the rapid deceleration of the accident, meant that the driver also suffered whiplash injuries to his neck, and a dislocated shoulder. Small reported that Rawnsley-Bysh was conscious as they loaded him into an ambulance for the journey to hospital in Palermo, and seemed in reasonably good spirits.

Piers Furnley continued to hold the gap to the first placed Ferrari at around one minute thirty seconds, but in third place Fondi relentlessly closed until he was right behind the Pegasus. Enthralling as this was for the spectators they eagerly awaited a resumption of the duel between Nalbandian and Snelgrove and at approaching 4pm in the afternoon the cars once more headed for pit lane.

Faletti swung the lead Ferrari through the final corner and into pit lane, growled past the Pegasus crew and pulled up in front of the Cordoba pit. Faletti leapt out while Nalbandian waited to replace him, and mechanics waited impatiently to change the wheels. Hammers clanged against central wheel nuts and three spun loose, but the fourth, the right rear, stuck. Trying the keep calm, the unfortunate mechanic, upon whose head all manner of excitable Latin curses were now heaped, struck the wheel nut again but still it refused to budge. Precious seconds ticked by as the car remained stationary, although it was refuelled - but still the fourth wheel nut remained obstinately unmoved. All this was too much for Don Pietro, who waved his arms and screamed in a most un-aristocratic manner, while Nalbandian paced back and forth. Team manager Castellotti stepped forward, grabbed the hammer, barged the mechanic unceremoniously out of the way and gave the wheel nut a mighty 'thwack', but to no effect.

Outside the Pegasus pit Charlie Small and Freddie Kendal jumped up and down with unconcealed excitement. "They've got a problem!" yelled Freddie, "they can't get the right rear wheel off!" Charlie Small turned on his heel, "come one Piers!" he yelled, although the dark green car was nowhere yet to be seen, "where the bloody hell are you!" Peter Snelgrove emerged from the rear of the garage already helmeted and gloved and now stood waiting, arms folded, fingers of his left hand nervously tap tapping his right arm. Finally the Pegasus roared into pit lane with the second Ferrari close behind. Furnley pulled up before the Pegasus pit and leapt out, pulling off his helmet as mechanics set-to changing wheels and fuelling the car.   "What...?" he began, pointing towards the Cordoba pit.

Castellotti gave the offending wheel nut another mighty crack, and this time it loosened almost easily, as if wondering what all the fuss was about.   Quickly trolley jacks were under the car, wheels changed, and the car returned to terra firma.   Nalbandian stepped quickly over the door and slid into the driver's seat, buckled up his seat belt, started the engine and was away; while down in the Pegasus pit Snelgrove was ready, the car was ready, and he too charged out of pit lane.   Watching from the grandstand opposite, spectators were on their feet with excitement, certain now that they were in for a race to the finish.   Held up for precious seconds while the first Ferrari was readied for the race, Fondi pulled the second car into the pit and in double-quick time Von Schmidt was in the driver's seat and in hot pursuit, not the least bit phased by the two cars ahead of him, and determined to win the race himself.

As the three cars streaked up the gentle incline to Cerda with not much more than four seconds between Nalbandian in first place and Von Schmidt in third, spots of rain began to fall as the first of the anticipated showers made a late afternoon appearance.   Placing his car practically on the lead Ferrari's rear bumper, Snelgrove watched for an opening but Nalbandian appeared untroubled by the shower until the three car 'train' approached the left hand sweep downhill onto 'Mussolini's road'.   As the cars neared the corner the rain fell much harder, the Argentinean hesitated and for a fraction of a second lifted off the accelerator.   Snelgrove grabbed the chance with both hands and swept around the Ferrari on the outside of the bend to take the lead. Behind him Von Schmidt tried the same manoeuvre but Nalbandian recovered quickly and although the two Ferraris were briefly side by side, Von Schmidt was forced to drop back as he had to take to the grass verge and found himself a few narrow centimetres from an unyielding stone wall.

In the pits area the shower arrived just as quickly, and glancing out of the garage to assess how long it might last, Brookes noticed Nicola jumping up and down in the rain with excitement as she listened to the tannoy. Splashing her way back to the garage, she burst in with the news: "he's done it!" she shrieked, "Peter's got by Nalbandian, he's leading the race!" Mike Brookes jaw dropped in amazement and the rest of the pit erupted, mechanics shaking hands and slapping each other on the back, Charles Standish and Archibald Drew talking animatedly to each other. Quickly Brookes snapped out of it. "Hold it!" he yelled, "we haven't won the race yet, there are still three and a half laps left, that's one-and-a-half hours of racing, almost the length of a Grand Prix and a lot can happen in that time. Now, you all know that Peter has to come in again for another set of tyres so make sure everything is ready because if any of you screw up that last stop I'll have your balls! Now get on with it!" Duly returned to earth the crew went about their assignments, but with barely suppressed anticipation over what the next couple of hours might bring.

In the Cordoba pit the atmosphere was also electric with anticipation. Don Pietro raged and fumed as he heard that Snelgrove was through, and erupted sufficient to embarrass Mt. Etna when news came over the tannoy that Von Schmidt was also attempting to get by Nalbandian. "What's he doing!?" the Don raged at the unfortunate Castellotti, "he'll have both our cars off if he carries on like that!"

Out on the circuit conditions were grim, especially for open topped cars like the Pegasus Seafire and the Ferrari Testa Rossas. While the cars travelled at speed their momentum swept rain from the visors on the drivers helmets, but in slower corners raindrops splashed and ran down the perspex, blurring vision, obscuring braking and clipping points, and made even the road surface itself indistinct. As the rain slackened, Jorge Nalbandian recovered his confidence and began to pull away from his team mate, setting off in pursuit of the disappearing Peter Snelgrove. Struggling mightily to stay in contact Von Schmidt slammed his car tight into a left hand bend on the approach to Campofelice just as the setting sun burst through a gap in the clouds. Blinded by the glare of the sun on his wet visor, Von Schmidt missed his clipping point and braked hard, spinning the car around. Out of control, the Ferrari hit a kerb broadside on and lifted, turning lazily in the air before crashing to earth upside down at the side of the road. In the cockpit the German ace had the presence of mind both to duck down and switch off the ignition before the car landed. The contours of the rear bodywork of the Ferrari curved up in graceful lines to outline the shape of the driver's head as he sat at the wheel, and it was this raised section that now held the back of the car off the ground and prevented Von Schmidt from being crushed. He was, however, well and truly trapped and sat, upside down in the silence, listening to the tap tapping of raindrops on the bodywork of the car.

To Von Schmidt it seemed that he must have remained in that cramped prison for an age and it was with some relief that he first heard voices and then watched as a number of pairs of feet gathered around the car. Voices chattered and argued in Italian and finally the car began to move, initially up onto its side and then with a crash over on its wheels once more. Von Schmidt raised his head and his saviours, spectators who had seen the crash, all began to talk to him at once. Driving for an Italian team the German had a smattering of Italian but this was all much too rapid for him, however he did gather that they were pleased to see that body and soul were still together. Carefully the driver undid the seatbelt, opened the car door and stepped out. No bones appeared to be broken and slowly at first, then more quickly as his confidence grew, he walked around as the spectators stood watching, clapping and shouting encouragement. Then he turned to look at the car. There was no doubt that the beautiful machine looked a shade second hand, its top bodywork badly dented and battered. He glanced sideways to the man standing at his right, a Sicilian farmer, puffing laconically on a pipe of evil smelling tobacco. The man looked at him and shook his head, his face a picture of dejected gloom. Beneath the visor Von Schmidt licked his lips then walked slowly back to the car and sat back in the driver's seat as a hushed and expectant silence fell over the assembled company. Carefully he turned the ignition and to his surprise and delight the engine fired. Quickly he refastened the seatbelt, slammed the door shut and put the car in gear. Gently lifting off the clutch and feeding in the accelerator he neither heard or felt anything untoward, and so, waving a grateful adieu to his unbelieving but ecstatic rescuers, he edged the car back onto the road, accelerated hard and was back in the race.

Using all his skill and the opportunities presented to him by the wet/dry conditions and the failing light, Peter Snelgrove pulled out a lead of some minutes over Nalbandian, but it was along the 6 kilometre straight towards the end of his second lap that he felt that something was wrong, and not with the car.

In darkness now, cars roared by with headlights on, while along pit lane the steely glow from electric lights overhead cast harsh shadows. In the Pegasus pit, Mike Brookes glanced at his watch. "Peter should be here any second", he said. "What's happening now?" he asked Charlie Small, and the diminutive mechanic ducked out to look along pit road. "Nothing", he said, "doesn't look as if Cordoba are ready for a pit stop".
"OK", responded Brookes, "Von Schmidt didn't come in after his accident so we'll have to assume that they're both going through to the end now without another stop". Looking up he met Alan Francis gaze; "all ready?" he asked, and the engineer licked dry lips and nodded.

The Pegasus Seafire pulled to an untidy stop in front of the pit and mechanics swarmed around it, but in the car Peter Snelgrove slumped forward onto the steering wheel. "Peter!" called Nicola, and Brookes, standing at the front of the car, looked up. Arriving at the driver's side, Brookes lifted him gently back in the seat. "Peter", he asked, "what is it?"

"Chest", mumbled Snelgrove, "terrible pains in my chest". Brookes motioned urgently for help and Both Freddie Kendal and Charlie Small helped him lift the recumbent driver out of the car and into the pit, where he was laid on the floor. Brookes knelt by the driver, placed rolled up overalls under his head and gently lifted off the silver helmet. "Don't worry", he said, "we'll get you to hospital". Snelgrove's eyes flickered open and he licked his lips, tried to focus and tried to speak. Brookes stood, turned and found Nicola standing behind him. Firmly she thrust the claret coloured racing helmet and his driving gloves against his chest. "Get in the car", she said, her unflinching gaze looking him straight in the eyes, "drive!" Brookes blinked, momentarily uncomprehending. "Peter", he responded, "we have to..."

"*We'll* get him to hospital", she continued, "*you* drive the car. Peter's given you the chance to win this damn race. Nalbandian will be along any second and neither of the other drivers has a chance of beating him, but you might. Get in the car", she repeated in a tone that would not tolerate argument, "and drive!"

"Car's ready guv", said Charlie Small, standing beside him, "fuelled, new tyres, ready to go". Quickly Brookes snatched the helmet, pulled it on, buckled the chinstrap, and taking his gloves, knelt again beside Snelgrove. The stricken driver looked up at him and managed the glimmer of a smile. "He's good", he said quietly, "no bloody pushover, but he's not too keen on the rain or night driving. Follow your own advice, keep him rattled, don't let him settle. You can take him..."

Standing by the car Freddie Kendal studied his watch. "He'll be here any second!" he yelled urgently and Brookes stood and sprinted for the car, vaulting into the driver's seat and waiting while Kendal buckled up the harness. Seconds later the dark green Pegasus screeched off into the night.

As he left pit lane Brookes glanced in the mirror and was certain he saw the headlights of the Ferrari round the corner and follow him across the start/finish line. Seconds later he was certain as the cherry red machine attempted to get alongside while Brookes was still building up speed. Up the incline towards Cerda Nalbandian weaved from side to side in his attempts to get by and Brookes had his work cut out keeping the Argentinean behind him while at the same time finding his own way past a number of slower back markers. Through the narrow streets of the village the two cars screamed nose to tail, while ecstatic Sicilians yelled encouragement to both drivers from their balconies above the road.

Up the twisting track to the heights of Caltavatura and through the left hand sweep onto 'Mussolini's' road Nalbandian tried everything he knew to get by. Approaching the village of Collesano Brookes remembered the sharp left hand hairpin, but fractionally misjudging his approach got onto lose pebbles and stones on the outside of the corner and slid wide, clipping the stone wall boundary with the right rear wing of the car. It was enough for Nalbandian who was through on the inside and into the lead, while Brookes, cursing himself for making such a bloody silly mistake, hared off in pursuit.

For the remainder of that lap, with a drying track, Nalbandian made the most of his lead and pulled slowly away despite everything that Brookes could do. Across the start/finish line and into the last lap of the race Nalbandian was something over one minute ahead and, cheered to the echo by the Cordoba pit and the crowds in the grandstand, poised for his and Cordoba's first Targa victory. Up through Cerda and into the mountains the two cars sped, and then the rain returned, a light drizzle at first but becoming harder. In the dry Nalbandian's tyres performed well, despite being three laps old, but in the wet they began to show their age. In the second place Pegasus Brookes sensed the smallest of chances as the gap to the leader at first stabilised and then steadily if slowly began to reduce. Bursting through the village of Campofelice the gap was under thirty seconds, but all that remained of the lap was the 6 kilometre straight and the final corner to the chequered flag. Brookes knew that even if he could get right up to the hard charging Argentinean his chances of getting by were minimal. Unless... An idea filed away in the back of his mind was suddenly crystal clear, and as he watched the Ferrari ahead make its turn and disappear onto the straight he switched off the Seafire's lights.

Seconds after the Ferrari, the Seafire swung onto the straight, street lighting practically non-existent, high roadside hedges darkening the narrow tarmac stretching ahead of him, a ribbon of road in the moonlight. Slamming his foot down hard on the accelerator Brookes felt the car surge forward, while up ahead he could see the tail lights of the Ferrari. With the undulating surface of the road bucking the car first towards the waiting jaws of a storm drain on one side of the road and then the other, with tyres slithering and scrabbling for grip, Brookes kept up his relentless pace and saw the brake lights of the Ferrari come on as it crossed the bridge. Nalbandian had not braked there on the last lap. He must think he had the race in the bag. Coming to the bridge himself Brookes kept the accelerator to the floor. The ramp for the bridge was not of any great note but it was still enough to have all four wheels of the Pegasus off the road, the car landing with a slithering crunch. Now, with the Cordoba Ferrari directly ahead, Brookes switched on the lights. Caught completely by surprise, Nalbandian lost concentration for the fraction of a second that it took for the Pegasus to muscle its way up on the inside.. Briefly the cars touched in a shower of sparks and then the dark green car was in front and across the line to win by half a bonnet's length after almost eight hours of racing.

Brookes brought the car to a halt and his mind swirled with the events of the last few moments. As he tried to focus, members of the Pegasus crew were leaping over the pit wall, meeting enthusiastic Sicilian race goers at the car, lifting him bodily from it and carrying him shoulder high towards the dais where Vincenzo Florio waited, smiling broadly and clapping enthusiastically, to present the trophy, the famous shield, the Targa. Looking around in something of a daze, Brookes firstly noticed that Jorge Nalbandian was being accorded the same treatment, and that was as it should be. The Sicilians had witnessed a classic motor race, one of the greats, and now flooded the track to show their appreciation, blocking the way for the third placed Jaguar, and Von Schmidt in fourth. Looking down, Brookes sought out a familiar face and found Charlie Small close by in the crowd. "Peter?", Brookes shouted over the tumult, "how is he?"
"In hospital in Palermo", Charlie shouted back, "Nicola and George Stepanek are with him, they'll call us here if

anything happens". With further conversation impossible, Brookes removed his helmet and gloves and allowed himself to be carried to the platform and hefted aboard. Smiling broadly Vincenzo Florio shook his hand warmly as Jorge Nalbandian was deposited next to the Pegasus boss by the wildly enthusiastic crowd. Uncertain of the response he would get, Brookes turned and held out his hand to the Argentinean. "Great race", said the Englishman, "you drove brilliantly". Nalbandian gave a Latin shrug. "Not well enough", he replied, and smiled. "I think it will be as well to come to this race once per year" he continued, "otherwise a driver might begin to think that he is better than he is. I understand that Peter Snelgrove is unwell, is it serious?"

"I don't know" responded Brookes, "I hope not, this victory is his and the team's more than mine". The two men shook hands. "We shall race again Michael Brookes", said the Argentinean matter of factly, "and I will beat you next time".

"Not me you won't", smiled Brookes, "I know a lady that would have my balls for bangles if I ever went near a racing car again!"

With the presentations made and the all-important prize money cheque in his pocket, Mike Brookes declined interview requests for the time being and threaded his way back toward the pits through a still excited crowd, to an accompaniment of much back slapping and hand shaking.

It being no secret that both Peter Snelgrove and Andrew Rawnsley-Bysh recuperated at the same hospital, the scene outside when Charlie Small brought the Land Rover to a halt resembled rehearsals for a Busby Berkeley musical at which the great man was absent and the replacement choreographer was drunk. Flash bulbs popped and journalists from newspapers, magazines, radio and television, jostled, pushed, shoved and shouted in their attempts to get the first words and the best picture. Mike Brookes stepped down from the passenger seat and he and Charlie pushed their way through the throng, eventually making their way to the front door where Sicilian police held back the crowd to allow them through. Inside Brookes found Nicola and George Stepanek waiting for him. Rushing to him Nicola put her arms around his neck and hugged as though she had thought she might never see him again. "You did it!" she whispered, "you did it!" Gently he pushed her away and smiled. "I see you heard", he said. "It was all over the radio here in the hospital", she replied, "yes I heard". George Stepanek stepped forward and shook his hand, "well done", he said quietly. "It was Peter's race", said Brookes, "how are they?"

"Adrian dislocated a shoulder", Nicola replied, "and has a broken ankle, but he will be fine. They'll keep him here for a few days under observation, then they expect he'll be able to go home".

"And Peter?" Nicola bit her lip. "We don't know yet, a senior surgeon will meet us while we're here and tell us what they know".

"Alright", said Brookes, "let's go see them and hope the news isn't too bad".

"Yes", she said, and taking his arm led him, followed by Stepanek and Charlie Small, to see Rawnsley-Bysh.

They found the driver propped up in bed, his right leg supported by a sling. "Great drive", he said as Brookes entered, "shame I couldn't make it a one-two".

"Never mind that", replied the Pegasus boss, "how are you? Do you have everything you need?" Rawnsley-Bysh wrinkled his nose, "well", he said smiling, "wish I had taken Italian instead of French at the old alma mater, some of the nurses here are rather scrummy".

"Uh?" said Charlie, immediately all attention, and to general amusement. "Good, Adrian", Brookes said with genuine relief, "you're obviously not feeling too bad. We'll be around for a few days before pulling out so If they let you out of here in time we can go back together. As I expect you know, Peter was also brought in here, so as Nicola speaks the language she'll remain in Palermo for a time until we can see what needs to be done to get you both home. In the meantime there'll always be somebody around the hospital from the team, so if there's anything you need, get word to us. OK?"

""OK boss", replied the injured driver, and as the visitors turned to leave he called them back. "How is Peter", he asked, "I can't find out what's happening".

"He was taken ill during the race", Nicola replied. "We don't know much more ourselves but we're just going to find out, we'll let you know".

"That was a hell of a drive he put in", said the driver admiringly. "Yes", agreed Brookes, "it was a hell of a drive".

Making their way up to the next floor of the hospital and the intensive care unit, the group were met by the senior surgeon, with whom Nicola conversed for some moments before turning her attention back to her companions. "They think", she said, "that Peter has had a heart condition developing for some time, but that he was probably not aware of it. Unfortunately the race was too much for him and he suffered an attack".

"But he will be OK?" asked Brookes anxiously. Nicola nodded. "With rest and proper care", she replied, "they expect him to make a decent recovery but of course he will never drive again". Brookes recalled the fire of determination seen in Peter Snelgrove's eyes only hours previously and was immensely saddened by the news, even though deep down he expected it. Seeing Brookes stricken expression, Stepanek laid a hand gently on his arm. "After the war", he said, "Peter really wanted to race again, but Chinese whispers ensured that nobody would give him a chance. He told me before the race that the Pegasus drive gave him back his self respect; I thank you for that and so will he". Nicola asked if they might see the driver and the surgeon agreed, provided they did not stay too long or over-excite the patient.

Entering the private ward the visitors found Snelgrove lying in bed with his head propped up on a pillow. Turning to them the smile he gave was small but genuinely meant, and reflected in his eyes. "Well done, Mike", he said.

"You heard?" responded Brookes, a little surprised. "As soon as they brought me round it was the first thing I asked", replied Snelgrove. "The race was on the radio, but as I don't speak Italian I had the doctor translate for me". The driver smiled. "He was getting quite excited", he continued and smiled ruefully. "I think he's a Ferrari fan. He was quite crestfallen when you snatched the win at the line".

"I was lucky", said Brookes, and Snelgrove sniffed. "Lucky hell", he said, "it took me a few minutes to figure out how you managed to make up so much ground down that straight, then I had it. You switched the lights off didn't you? You went down that bloody straight with no lights on so he thought you'd gone off and took his foot off the gas".

"WHAT!" Exclaimed Nicola, "you did *WHAT!*"

"Umm, well, I er...." Nicola stood silent but fuming, arms folded. Standing with George Stepanek across the bed from the pair, Charlie caught Brookes glance and grimaced. The boss was going to catch hell for this and they both knew it. "It was your win", said Brookes genuinely, "if you hadn't driven the way you did we wouldn't have had a chance".

"Well, I don't think I'd have done what you did", Snelgrove replied, and this time Brookes sniffed. "You wouldn't have had to", he said, "you wouldn't have let the bugger get past in the first place".

"Maybe, maybe not", said Snelgrove, "just save some champers for me, OK?" All four of the visitors chorused their approval, a noise which brought the surgeon in hot foot to usher them out of the room lest they over exert the patient.

Relieved that both drivers appeared to be on the mend, the four returned to their hotel. Alone in their room, Nicola did indeed give Brookes hell, but she was not really angry, just relieving nervous tension, and when she calmed down she put her arms around him, made him swear never to drive a racing car again, and took him to bed.

Dawn the following morning was chilly and overcast. Alan Francis and the team, many among their number sporting jumbo-sized hangovers, set about packing up their gear for the journey home. Charlie had not yet put in an appearance and the hot rumour was that he had managed to track down the pretty little hotel receptionist.

Standing on the start-finish line, Mike Brookes smiled to himself. He had popped the question to Nicola the previous night and she tearfully accepted. Now he gazed out along the silent road as bits of bunting and food wrappers swirled and blew in the breeze, and in the stands work on the post race clear up began. Brookes took a deep breath, and thrusting hands in pockets he turned to walk slowly back to the pits.

Acknowledgements

With thanks to all my friends, who patiently put up with me being a complete pain in the neck about my writing.

TOK258 – Morgan Winner at Le Mans

By Ronnie Price

"I would recommend this book to anyone. It is the story of how skill and personal determination can beat the most elaborate, expensive and sophisticated machinery, the story of David versus Goliath. I warmly hope that it inspires the reader to try and achieve their own personal dreams"

Charles Morgan

Chairman, Morgan Car Company

Lightning Source UK Ltd.
Milton Keynes UK
09 August 2010

158125UK00001B/21/P